Praise for B

Rob Acton provides the definitive road map for a busy professional to find and serve their cause. A must read for anyone eager to make an impact in the world!

Karamo Brown,
Emmy Award Winning Television Host, Producer, and Activist

Rob's book is a powerful companion to the traditional management books sought out by corporate leaders. He reminds us that even the busiest, most successful professionals are more effective and content when connected to the broader community and leveraging their skills for social causes meaningful to them. And even better, Rob offers clear direction on how to make it happen.

Ed Wells,
CEO, The Second City

Rob Acton's book shares foundational insights into how successful professionals can find success in driving societal change. Whether you're decades into your career or just embarking upon it, *Becoming a Causie* is an essential guide for charting your path to impact in tandem with growth in the workplace.

Steve Beard,
President & CEO, Adtalem Global Education

The time is now for nonprofit board service to be promoted and marketed to corporations, organizations, and individuals as the extraordinary opportunity it is. Rob makes a very powerful case. The stories he shares should propel each one of us to get off the bench and onto the field.

Joan M. Garry,
Best-selling Author & Founder of the Nonprofit Leadership Lab

Acton's book is a game-changer for professionals looking to transition from success to significance. His insights and guidance offer a practical approach to finding purpose and making a difference in the world.

Juan Mejia,
President, New York Presbyterian / Brooklyn Methodist Hospital

Rob's passion for social impact is contagious, and *Becoming a Causie* is a testament to his commitment to helping others find purpose in serving their communities. Whether you're a seasoned executive or a young professional, this book will motivate and empower you to make a difference as a nonprofit board leader.

Matt Lashey,
Creator & CEO of Wave Health and CEO at Treatment Technologies & Insights, Inc.

The connection between our professional aspirations and personal passions does not need to exist in silos. Rob and his organization, Cause Strategy Partners, make this a reality by inspiring the workforce to pursue social good initiatives through the paradigms of skills and expertise. *Becoming a Causie* is insightful and thought provoking, begging the question, "What is your cause?" In it he defines what it means to be purpose-driven and helps readers unlock how we find deeper, intentional meaning in the work we do and the causes we support.

Shannon Schuyler,
U.S. Chief Purpose and Inclusion Officer, PwC

Have you ever wondered how to turn your passion into lasting purpose serving the nonprofit sector by becoming a board member extraordinaire? Written for incredibly busy people who eschew mediocrity in all they do, this indispensable how-to guide presents everything you need to know to serve *your* cause over your lifetime.

Dr. Cathy Trower,
Author & Principal of Trower & Trower, Inc.

Rob Acton's book is a game-changer for anyone seeking to leverage their skills for social good. With clarity and passion, Acton demystifies the path to nonprofit board leadership, offering actionable advice and compelling insights. *Becoming a Causie* is more than a book; it's a catalyst for meaningful change in our communities and beyond.

Brandon Parkes,
Founder & CEO, Parkes Philanthropy

Rob brilliantly provides a road map for anyone who wants to be a Causie! Sharing direct experiences, insights, advice and yes, even questions to consider, this approach creates a path for anyone wanting to engage in meaningful nonprofit board service.

Lisa Dietlin,
Author & CEO of the Institute of Transformational Philanthropy

If you have a burning desire to make a difference but are unsure how to harness it into action, Rob's book is the antidote. He shows you how to mobilize that interest and channel it into meaningful board service. Rob is one of our country's most experienced guides for professionals wanting to step into board service. This long-awaited resource has tremendous potential to catalyze and scale talent into governance roles in the social good sector.

Dr. Laura Zumdahl,
President & CEO, New Moms

Becoming a Causie is a must read for anyone who has wondered how to be an impactful board member. Rob Acton's deep understanding of effective nonprofit board service is evident on every page of this wonderful book. His guidance will not only help individuals learn how to live their purpose through meaningful board service, but it will also help to build a stronger nonprofit sector.

Gary Bagley,
Nonprofit Consultant and Adjunct Professor of International and Public Affairs, Columbia University

"A must read for anyone ready to make an impact in the world!"
—**Karamo Brown**, Television Host and Activist

Becoming a Causie

Champion Your Cause
Through Nonprofit Board Leadership

Rob Acton
A Top 100 Impact CEO

Advantage | Books

Published by Advantage Books, Charleston, South Carolina.
An imprint of Advantage Media.

ADVANTAGE is a registered trademark, and the Advantage colophon is a trademark of Advantage Media Group, Inc.

Printed in the United States of America.

10 9 8 7 6 5 4 3 2 1

ISBN: 978-1-64225-722-9 (Paperback)
ISBN: 979-8-89188-196-9 (Hardcover)
ISBN: 978-1-64225-721-2 (eBook)

Library of Congress Control Number: 2024910521

Cover design by Lance Buckley.
Layout design by Wesley Strickland.

To Alexandra "Allie" Hallock—my dear friend and colleague, whose trust, dedication, and unwavering support have left an indelible mark on my life and our work at Cause Strategy Partners.

Contents

Acknowledgments

I want to express my deepest gratitude to those who have been most instrumental in shaping my values and strengthening my life's journey over the years.

To Bill and Jane Acton: My brothers and I have always known that—despite your successful and rewarding careers—you viewed the most important aspect of your life's work to be instilling in us a set of values that would lead to faithful, meaningful, and fulfilling lives.

To Jeff Acton and Kevin Acton: I've been blessed to have the example of two brothers to learn from, emulate, and follow, every day of my life.

To Thomas Durein, Scott Ashley, Matt Lashey, and Clinton Lewis: You've shown up every time I needed you, and you've provided more laughter, love, and support than a person should enjoy in a lifetime.

To my nieces and nephews—Jeffrey, Jamie, Leigha, Anthony, Mckenzie, Austin, Tyler, Kasey, Steve, Kelsey, K. Robert, and Lia—sister-in-law Cindy Acton, Uncle Jerry, Aunt Beth, and many more family members: Thank you for your love, constancy, belief, humor, and appreciation for playing board and card games long into the night.

To so many incredible friends who have enriched my life: You are too many to name, and you know who you are. I'm so thankful for each one of you.

To the Cause Strategy Partners Advisory Board—Matt Lashey, Leah Bradford Francis, Josh Edelman, Beth Gallagher, Myung Lee, Cullen Malley, Farissa Knox, Evans Legros, Eric Weng, Nathan Richardson, and Stacy Winter: Thank you for your encouragement to always make stretch moves. My sights have been raised because of you.

To my mentors at various stages of life—Rod Mathews, Dwight Robertson, Oreon Trickey, James B. O'Neal, Dr. Charles Middleton, and Sylvia Reynolds: You pointed me to destinations in my life's journey—and showed me pathways to get there—long before I could see them myself.

To Angela Grovey, Allen René Louis, Anna Kaltenbach, and the Broadway Inspirational Voices (BIV) board of directors and choir members: It is a gift to join each one of you in changing lives through the power of music and service. BIV is more than just an organization to me; you've become my family.

To Peter Sloane and the Heckscher Foundation for Children: I am eternally grateful for your confidence in me and for believing in the big idea I pitched to you in 2015. You allowed me to answer the question hanging on a sign in my office: "What would you do if you weren't afraid?"

This book would not have been possible without the help of a number of people who should also have their names on the cover.

To Mary Martin: The day we met, you promised that you'd "pull a book out of me." Mission accomplished, my friend. Your brilliance, patience, and encouragement got us to the finish line. Maybe, more importantly, I made a lifetime friend in the process.

To my editor, Nate Best, and the incredible team at Forbes Books|Advantage Media: I've only worked with one editor and publisher, but I can't imagine that there is a more capable group of professionals doing this work.

To Brandon Freeman, Carl Gaines, Kerri Catalano, Adam Stanley, Gretchen Slusser, James B. O'Neal, Jeremy Taylor, Lisa Dietlin, John Eric Parker, Nathan Richardson, Johnathan Lay, and many others whose stories I share on these pages: Thank you, friends.

To the host of outstanding board members I have been privileged to serve shoulder to shoulder with over the years: Thank you for setting an example of governance excellence. I have learned from you and have been inspired by you.

To our client liaisons, BoardLeaders, and nonprofit partners of Cause Strategy Partners: Individually, you make this work possible. Collectively, we are changing the very definition of what it means to be a nonprofit board leader. Many of your stories are told in this book, as well.

To Anakaren Cervantes: Working with you on MyCauseFinder was one of the most memorable aspects of this journey. Your expert collaboration skills, insightful ideas, and determined effort are the reason this tool exists. I'd build things again and again with you.

To Jono Warren, Cambri Wright, James Hannon, Nate Hinchey, and Jazmin Vega: Thank you for taking on added work assignments to help this book come to fruition.

To the CSP Leadership Team—Whitley Richards, Erin Pierson, and Erin Connell: Thank you for steering the ship so ably and especially during my writing sabbatical. You are a gift to me.

Finally, to the Causies whom I get to work alongside each day: Your dedication to our vision, mission, and values constantly inspires me and refuels my passion for our work. Any accolade for the success of Cause Strategy Partners is owed to you.

Introduction

I want my life to be something more than long.
—FROM THE TONY AWARD–WINNING MUSICAL *Pippin*

When you walk into a social setting—a friend's birthday party, a wedding reception, or a neighborhood bar, for example—you often encounter someone you've never met before. Unless you forgo all social conventions, both of you likely feel an obligation to say something to one another.

After shaking hands and exchanging names, there's a familiar go-to question that usually gets asked next. *"So, what do you do for a living?"*

In January 2012, what I did for a living was pretty interesting, at least in my book. I was serving as the executive director of Taproot Foundation in New York City, a national organization that connects business professionals to nonprofits for pro bono consulting projects.

To spice up these unremarkable conversations and make them more meaningful, I made a 2012 New Year's resolution. I decided that when I was asked the question, "What do you do for a living?" I would share about my work at Taproot in support of hundreds of nonprofit organizations across the country. But instead of responding in kind, I would ask a different question: "Tell me, what causes do you support?" I was sure this would immediately energize the exchange and inspire shared connections.

I was wrong. In fact, it turned out to be a terribly awkward New Year's resolution. *Warning: Don't try this at home!* Most of these new acquaintances were caught completely flat-footed by my question. They would hem and haw, sometimes glancing upward while they searched for a response.

I often found myself coaching them in order to interrupt these uncomfortably long moments of introspection. "You know, where do you volunteer? Where do you make donations? Maybe you serve on a nonprofit board?" The most common response was a blank stare. I remember one gentleman—after pondering the question—looked at me quizzically and said, "Well I like TV a lot. Does that count?"

According to the Charities Aid Foundation's *World Giving Index*, 37 percent of Americans volunteered in 2021 and 67 percent donated money to charity.[1] So where, I wondered, was the disconnect? Was I hanging around with the wrong crowd? Was my network somehow filled with people who were self-centered, indifferent, and lacking in generosity as compared with the broader population?

I don't think that was it. Instead, I believe I was experiencing the fundamental difference between a passive approach and a purpose-driven approach to serving one's cause. A passive approach might result in an occasional donation to support a friend's social media campaign in support of their favorite charity. It might even lead to volunteering for a couple of hours at the local food pantry on Thanksgiving Day. Those are good things to do, to be sure, but they aren't transformative for the individual, the organization, or the cause.

---

[1] "CAF world giving index 2022," CAF, accessed March 26, 2024, https://www.cafonline.org/about-us/publications/2022-publications/caf-world-giving-index-2022.

A purpose-driven approach to finding and serving a cause is something very different. It has the potential to be personally life altering and create a life-sustaining impact for the beneficiaries of those the organization serves.

What I didn't anticipate at the time was that my New Year's resolution would help me define and crystallize my own passion. It would give me a new vision for my life's purpose. It would inspire me to quit my job and start a company laser-focused on connecting professionals to the cause that's right for them. I wanted to help busy, talented people—just like those I was meeting in 2012—find and serve their cause so that they could use their valuable time, their considerable talents, their carefully curated network, and their hard-earned resources to make an impact on the world.

In short, I wanted to help inspire and build a movement of Causies: people with demanding schedules and full lives who nonetheless choose to dedicate themselves to intentionally and meaningfully serving their cause over a lifetime. Not my cause. Not their employer's cause. Not their favorite politician's cause. A Causie is someone who makes an intentional, substantial, long-term commitment to serve their cause.

> **A Causie is someone who makes an intentional, substantial, long-term commitment to serve their cause.**

The purpose of this book is to help you find and serve *your* cause. That's the journey we are embarking on together.

A Causie Movement Is Born

When I founded my company, Cause Strategy Partners, in 2015, I wanted our employees to have a shared name. Nicknaming a team is known to have a positive effect on employee culture and cohesion, creating a sense of shared purpose and belonging. Google refers to its employees as Googlers. Salesforce team members are Trailblazers. Workday uses Workmates. Disney employees are Cast Members. The team at Rocket Mortgage, headquartered in Motown? Brilliantly, they are Rock Stars.

Sure beats "Associates," doesn't it?

It didn't take long for me to realize that a defining characteristic of the people associated with Cause Strategy Partners—our employees, our clients, our board candidates, and our nonprofit partners—share one overarching trait. All of us are passionate about a cause. Many of us have multiple causes. I sometimes joke that our team rarely comes across a cause that we don't get excited about.

Why? Because we are Causies.

I owe the idea for "Causies" to the Tony Award–winning Broadway musical *Newsies*, based on the 1992 Disney film of the same name. "Newsie" was the nickname given to a poor and sometimes homeless boy, as young as five years old, who sold newspapers in the late nineteenth century.

Did you know that these Newsies were required to buy the newspapers they sold from the likes of Joseph Pulitzer and William Randolph Hearst, and if they didn't sell all the papers, they weren't allowed to return the unsold ones for a refund and had to take the financial loss? The Newsies brought attention to the inhumane conditions of child labor and challenged the unfair business practices of publishing tycoons by going on strike in the summer of 1899. Over five thousand Newsies organized to fight their treatment and the terms of their financial agreements. The Newsies formed a union, marched, and even blocked the Brooklyn Bridge, demanding justice. They got their terms, and their fight was credited with bolstering the movement to change child labor laws.

Not only were these kids Newsies—they were Causies! But they didn't do it alone. Their plight was documented by an American photographer named Lewis Hine, who had already been using his camera to protest child labor by photographing children in mines, factories, and sweatshops. For years, as the photographer for the National Child Labor Committee, Hine urged Congress to address this horrendous treatment of children and get them into school, where they belonged. His photographs are widely recognized for their significant role in shaping the creation and reformation of child labor laws in the United States.

Hine's powerful and often haunting images exposed the harsh realities of child labor in the early twentieth century, helping to galvanize public support for change. Through his lens, Hine captured the faces and stories of the countless children who were forced to work long hours in dangerous conditions, sacrificing their health and education in the process. His work was instrumental in bringing attention to this important issue and inspiring legislative action. To this day, Hine's images serve as a powerful reminder of the ongoing struggle to protect the rights and well-being of children.

Lewis Hine was drawn to documenting injustices in service of social reform—to, as he was known for saying, "show the things that had to be corrected." He didn't have it on his business card at the time, but Lewis Hine was a Causie.

A Causie is on a mission. A Causie sees a need and has to do something about it. A Causie commits to a purpose larger than themselves. A Causie makes service an important part of their personal and professional journey. To borrow from the musical *Pippin*, a Causie feels compelled to make their life "something more than long."

You're going to meet a lot of Causies in this book. They're all busy people immersed in the whirlwind of life, just like you and me. Each one is a working professional with a demanding job, loved ones to look after, friendships to enjoy, a home to maintain, and lots of outside interests to pursue. Yet each one also recognizes that serving their cause has to be part of their life's story, as well. Among others, you'll meet the following:

- Carl Gaines, head of content and media at Lument, who serves on the board of directors of Callen-Lorde Community Health Center—the same organization that provided him with free healthcare services years earlier as a vulnerable young gay man who had just moved to New York City without family support.

- Kerri Catalano, global head of recruiting at a financial and media company, who witnessed firsthand the damage that bullying caused her twin brother in their middle school years. She felt inspired to change that for kids growing up facing similar situations. Kerri discovered Beyond Differences, a nonprofit that addresses her cause and, in doing so, says she "found her purpose." She's been a rock star board member ever since.

- Gretchen Slusser, who went from global IT consultant to the executive director of Cabrini Green Legal Aid (CGLA) in Chicago with the help of Adam Stanley, a former senior executive in the C-suite of a global commercial real estate company turned entrepreneur turned board member extraordinaire. Their inspiring story is a powerful combination of passion, integrity, and serendipity.

Along with many more you'll soon meet, these Causies prove that it can be done. It's possible to have a big job and a big life while carving out space to serve one's cause. In fact, if you had the chance to ask them directly, I am certain they'd say that they would have it no other way.

I've heard lots of objections from people over the years who feel like they can't make a meaningful difference in society. Busyness, to be sure, is at the top of that list. But there are many more.

- I don't know anything about the nonprofit sector. I've only worked in business.

- That stuff is for bleeding-heart liberals, not capitalists like me.

- I don't have anything to offer. My skills wouldn't be useful.

- I don't have a lot of money. Serving on a board is for the rich.

- Sounds interesting, but I wouldn't know where to begin.

These dissents miss the mark. These barriers can all be overcome. And these mindsets misunderstand the purpose of the social good sector.

This book is designed to be a road map for busy professionals to get off the bench and onto the field—serving the community. Everyone should find and serve their cause. As Muhammad Ali once said, "Service is the rent you pay for a room on this Earth."

An Overview of What's Coming

We'll begin in chapter 1 with my story. Perhaps my experience will provide you with some inspiration and guidance on finding and serving your cause. I'll share about my journey as a founder and social entrepreneur, as well, and how the work we do at Cause Strategy Partners came to life.

Chapter 2 is your starting point for this journey as you discover your cause. You'll spend time with a set of exploratory questions, and you'll discover a free online quiz called *MyCauseFinder* to help you define your cause.

With your cause area now clear, chapter 3 will guide you in the process of uncovering the right organization for you to support and serve. We'll explore the various ways you can make an impact on a nonprofit organization that resonates with you.

In chapter 4, we'll examine what nonprofit board service is and help you weigh whether it's right for you. Chapter 5 will describe an elevated approach to nonprofit governance: we call it *The BoardLeader Way*.

Chapter 6 is your comprehensive guidebook for securing a seat on the board. We'll delve into the details, starting from the moment you and your target nonprofit's leadership agree to discuss a board seat, progressing to the introductory meeting, on to the site visit, and culminating with the decision of whether to stand for nomination as a member of the board of directors.

Chapter 7 shares best practices for starting strong as a new board member. You'll learn about the duties of board members, the delicate relationship with the executive director, and you'll be introduced to seven board member archetypes.

Chapter 8 demystifies the area that often instills the greatest apprehension among board members: fundraising. When you're finished with this chapter, you'll understand why most of your terror was misplaced, and you might even be excited to get out there and raise money for your cause.

Finally, in chapter 9, we explore the "big hairy audacious goal" (to borrow from Jim Collins in *Built to Last*) behind this work. How can we collectively elevate and transform governance in the nonprofit sector through a Causie Movement?

By being intentional about examining your values, defining your desired impact on the world, understanding your unique strengths that can contribute to the social impact sector, and carefully considering the many cause areas and organizations you might serve, I assure you that the perfect match is out there for you. My firm, Cause Strategy Partners, has placed thousands of professionals on nonprofit boards across the United States and the United Kingdom. We have witnessed firsthand—over and over again—the power of seeing someone find, serve, and drive impact on their cause. If you're ready to apply your wisdom, experience, professional skills, and resources toward making a positive impact on your community, nation, or the world, this book will serve as the bridge to help you get started today.

Living life as a Causie shapes who you are and how you move through the world. It becomes part of your identity. It's a core aspect of your story. In the not-too-distant future, when you meet a new acquaintance at a social gathering, I hope you'll tell them what you do for a living and then add in the cause that you support.

> *Hi, I'm Rob. I'm the founder and CEO of a consulting firm called Cause Strategy Partners. We place, train, and support business professionals for nonprofit board service. I also serve as board chair of a New York City nonprofit called Broadway Inspirational Voices, a diverse choir of Broadway artists united to change lives through the power of music and service. What about you? What do you do for a living and what causes do you support?*

See, it's not difficult at all when you're a Causie.

Chapter
One

My Causie Story

In our origins lie the seeds of our potential.
—UNKNOWN

I was raised in a close-knit, middle-class family in Davison, Michigan, a small town of only a few thousand residents located just fifteen minutes from Downtown Flint, a city that has sadly gained notoriety in recent years because of the discovery of lead contamination in the city's water supply, rendering it unsafe to drink since 2014.

My dad, Bill Acton, was a small-town minister who transitioned mid-career to become the founding executive director of a nonprofit camp called Covenant Hills, located twenty minutes from our home. Dad's career change was good for me. Spending every summer day and most weekends as the "camp brat"—running around the grounds as though I owned the place—was a great way to do childhood. This setup had it all for a precocious, energetic boy: fishing, canoeing, archery, skeet shooting, driving tractors, riding horses, exploring the wilderness, and collecting pet turtles. My dad also served as a Davison city council member and mayor pro tem for a period of time. I remember going door to door with him as a child campaigning, meeting neighbors, shaking hands, and asking for their vote.

Jane Acton, my mom, was a public high school English teacher and a dedicated, lifelong member of our town's Free Methodist Church. Mom grew up in Davison and never left: her deep commitment to her town, her school, her students, and her church was unwavering. After teaching all day, Mom would continue to work long hours on weekday evenings: grading papers, calling parents, and preparing lessons. I observed what hard work looked like as she gave her all to her students, both in and out of the classroom.

Both of my parents modeled service to the community and a commitment to their cause, each and every day. But there was one very noticeable thing missing in my upbringing: racial diversity. While Flint's population consisted of a large black community just a few exits west on Interstate 69, it might as well have been a world away from my childhood in Davison. The population of my town was virtually all white, the kids I went to church and to camp with were all white, and my "village"—the scores of loving adults who helped raise me—were all white, as well.

One day, my parents brought a set of comic books home for my two older brothers and me. The Spire Christian comic book series featured "heroes of the faith," including Brother Andrew (who snuck Bibles into communist countries), David Wilkerson (who reached out to street gangs), and the NFL football coach Tom Landry. But there was one comic book in the series that captivated me the most at a young age: *Tom Skinner up from Harlem.* This "hero" didn't look like all the others in the comic book series: he was black.

His story was different too, described by the publisher as a "Malcolm-X-like transformation from street gang member to religious leader." This comic book dramatized Tom Skinner's life growing up surrounded by racism, violence, and poverty. As an eight-year-old boy, I had found a role model. So much so, in fact, that I wrote Tom

Skinner a letter that my mom duly copied and is now saved in my childhood scrapbook.

> *Dear Tom Skinner, I read one of your comic books and I really liked it. I read Tom Skinner Up From Harlem. If that story is true, you must be brave. You must be famuse [sic]. My name is Robbie Acton. I'm almost 9. November 26 is my birthday. I'm not brown but brown people are as good as white. And I really like to make friends. I've got to stop writing now.*

I ended my letter with a request for Tom Skinner to "write or call me," and he did! I received a box of goodies from him a few weeks later.

Another letter that my mom preserved in my childhood scrapbook is from Judge Charles B. Mosier, a former jurist in Genesee County, sitting on the bench in Flint, Michigan. He wrote to six-year-old Robbie:

> *I received your letter about the wild stallions and your picture of a horse at the bottom of the letter. I certainly agree with you that horse meat does not sound very good and I will tell anyone interested that they should not kill wild stallions because I personally believe you are absolutely correct. I appreciate the time you took to write to me and I am now placing your letter in my book along with others I have received from fine young men like you who have an interest in animals and their safety.*

I took up the cause of Mothers against Drunk Driving (or MADD) during high school, making a speech at a school assembly. I wrote an opinion piece for the *Flint Journal* when I felt my school was under attack. It seems that, as soon as I could read and write, I had causes. Throughout my childhood and teenage years, I despised unfairness and injustice, and I translated those feelings into action. But it was in college that I began to home in on a primary cause.

I attended Spring Arbor University in Michigan, a modest-sized private college previously attended by my grandfather, parents, and both of my brothers. It was always assumed that I would attend Spring Arbor too. During my sophomore year, I joined a spring break service trip to Camden, New Jersey—a city of 74,000 residents across the Delaware River from Philadelphia. Camden has a long history of industrial and economic activity but has also faced significant challenges over the years, including high crime rates, poverty, and a struggling economy.

I boarded a college van to head to Camden in the spring of 1989 unaware of how the weeklong experience would shape the trajectory of the rest of my life. As we entered Camden's city limits, I remember an uncharacteristic silence settling in among the fourteen students in the van. For most of us—certainly for me—this was our first personal encounter with urban decay of that magnitude: boarded-up stores, broken roads and sidewalks, drug use in the open, and people living on the streets. At one point, we saw someone running down the street, pistol in hand.

Our assignment that week was to help run an afterschool program operating out of the basement of a church in the heart of Camden. As we tutored kids, led high-energy rallies, prepared lunches, wrote songs, visited families, and walked the city streets, moment by moment I felt my purpose crystallizing. I was deeply drawn to the vibrancy of the city despite its challenges. I was soaking in the opportunity to experience and learn about cultures very different from my own. I was inspired by the resilience of the neighborhood children and families.

The program's director, Dr. Bruce Main, must have sensed the evolution happening in my life. Toward the end of the week, Bruce took me to lunch. He pulled out a handful of coins to pay for two pizza slices. I recall him saying, "This is all I've got, but let's eat up!" As we talked over those slices, he challenged me to build on the personal awakening I was experiencing by returning to Camden in a few months for an unpaid, full-time, summer-long internship. And I did.

When I returned to Michigan for my junior year of college, I had clarity on my purpose: I would live and work in a low-income urban environment, championing more opportunities for young people caught in the cycle of poverty. This clarity, however, soon bumped up against the reality of student life—studying and attending classes. I wanted to be fulfilling my purpose, in the game, *now.* I set up a meeting with my academic advisor, Dr. Robert Bailey, to talk through what it would look like to drop out of school and begin to work in the community, full-time. He wisely counseled me to look for opportunities to nurture my purpose during the remaining two years of my undergraduate education rather than quit school and go back to Camden.

The very next week—in the fall of 1989—I drove down Frances Street in nearby Jackson, Michigan. Spring Arbor was majority white; the neighborhood surrounding Frances Street was majority black. Spring Arbor was well resourced and populated by academics and students. Frances Street was burdened with the all-too-familiar challenges faced by low-income urban neighborhoods. I stopped my car at the first church I encountered on Frances Street, knocked on the door, and was greeted by an imposing figure: the very tall, black, regal, senior pastor of a United Methodist Church serving the community.

Stumbling over my words as we stood on opposite sides of the doorway, I tried to quickly explain the program I'd participated in while in Camden, New Jersey, and asked if we might be able to use the pastor's church for a similar afterschool program called, "Action

Jackson." The pastor looked this scrawny nineteen-year-old college kid up and down, thought for a moment, smiled slightly, and then responded, "Let's give it a try."

Action Jackson quickly became the dominant part of my final two years of college. The program grew rapidly with more than 150 neighborhood kids attending every Tuesday and Thursday. Each week, I'd head back to campus and recruit my college classmates to help run the program.

The Frances Street community became an important part of my life. Upon graduation, I moved into the neighborhood, continuing to learn a great deal. I especially began to understand my own personal limitations in being useful. For example, I didn't know how to support one of our students whose mother was being abused at home when he knocked on my apartment door to ask for help. Furthermore, I wasn't of any use when one of our students was kicked out of school and his mom asked for my help in trying to get him re-enrolled. And I felt woefully inadequate trying to work toward systemic change when I found myself fumbling through testimony before the Jackson city council while petitioning for more community resources.

I began to understand that creating a broader, more significant impact needed to become my focus. I wanted to provide meaningful and lasting change for communities. This realization led me to apply to law school as a public interest fellow, and it took me to New York City. In the summer of 1994, I began studying at Brooklyn Law School.

My purpose was clear. I was awarded two public interest law fellowships during my law school years. The first was a paid internship at Covenant House Legal Services, which provided free legal services to homeless and trafficked youth. The second was a summer fellowship at the East Harlem Youth and Family Justice Center. After graduating and passing the New York State Bar exam, I took a position as the director of legal education at Legal Outreach, a powerful organization founded by one of my mentors and heroes, James B. O'Neal. Legal Outreach provides academic and social support to low-income, mostly minority and first-generation youth attending under-resourced schools in New York City. I served as a practicing attorney for a time, as well, representing children in abuse and neglect proceedings in Brooklyn Family Court.

Throughout my career, I've found that sometimes a job description would speak directly to me. Maybe that has happened to you too—after reading the job posting you think to yourself, "That job has to be mine." That was my experience when I read about the executive director role at Cabrini Green Legal Aid (CGLA) in Chicago. Legal assistance organizations like CGLA provide a variety of no-cost or low-cost legal services to the community's underserved, low-income, and marginalized populations, including those living in poverty, the elderly, foster children, families affected by domestic violence, the formerly incarcerated, and immigrants. CGLA was founded in the basement of LaSalle Street Church in Chicago. Serving as the chief executive of a nonprofit—walking in the footsteps of my dad—had always been a career goal of mine.

Despite reservations about leaving New York City, I applied for the position and soon found myself in Chicago, sitting for an interview with the organization's board of directors. I was struck by the reality that, as much as I might know about the law, leadership, and community service, I knew absolutely nothing about working for a board. In every previous job, I had one boss. In this role, I'd have ten!

A barrage of questions started flying through my mind:

- *How could I succeed in a role reporting to a host of people with varying opinions?*

- *What would be their responsibilities versus mine? And would they respect those boundaries?*

- *How could I engage the board in ways that advance the mission rather than mire them in too much detail?*

- *Did we have the right set of skills on the board to lead the organization effectively?*

- *What would be my relationship to the board chair versus the board as a whole?*

- *Why was the board—to be blunt—so white given that the organization served almost exclusively people of color?*

- *How quickly could we change the board's composition to better reflect the community we serve? How much sway might I have in pursuing this change?*

- *What was motivating our board members to serve in the first place?*

I accepted the job despite a number of concerns and uncertainties like these. And I'm glad I did. Serving as CGLA's executive director would prove to be a great laboratory of learning for me.

Seven years later, I was recruited to lead Taproot Foundation's work in New York City. Taproot helps nonprofits build strong infrastructure with the pro bono assistance of skilled professionals by recruiting and facilitating teams of volunteers who contribute their skills in pro bono marketing, human resources, technology, and strategy projects.

The Birth of Cause Strategy Partners

A few years into my tenure at Taproot, I received an email from Peter Sloane, president of the Heckscher Foundation for Children, inviting me to the foundation's office for lunch. I had no idea why the foundation's president—whom I'd never met—would want to meet with me. Nonprofit leaders typically work through program officers in the grantmaking process, not directly with a foundation head, so my curiosity was piqued. Little did I know at the time that this lunch would alter the course of my life.

Heckscher Foundation for Children is located on the Upper East Side of Manhattan in an impressive building constructed and completed in 1903. The headquarters is a classic example of the prewar architectural style, with elegant details such as ornamental stonework and arched windows. The foundation's receptionist ushered me into the boardroom, and I was invited to take a seat in the middle of a large conference room table. Peter soon joined me and sat at the head of the table in a high-backed chair, some distance away. I was intimidated, to be sure.

After we exchanged pleasantries, Peter said, "Rob, here's why I called you in: I want Taproot to start a board placement program for young professionals. People like me—gray-haired, middle-aged guys—are constantly being asked to sit on the boards of nonprofits. But there are so many young people who have energy, drive, and so much to give. We need to develop an initiative to give them the opportunity. Can you build that?"

As enticing as the idea was, and as much as I wanted to dive in headfirst, I also recognized that board service fell outside of Taproot's core mission. The organization facilitates pro bono consulting projects, not board service. I was relatively sure that Taproot's board of directors wouldn't approve the engagement, viewing it instead as mission drift. I respectfully declined, and Peter and I parted ways. For a while.

Almost exactly a year later, Peter invited me back in for lunch. "Rob, do you remember when I asked you to start a board placement program?" he asked.

How could I forget? "Of course I do, Peter."

"Well, we ended up giving $125,000 to another organization to do the work. Care to guess how many board members they placed?"

I took a stab. "Seventy? Eighty?"

Peter formed a circle with his right hand.

Taken aback, I responded, "Wait, you awarded a $125,000 grant and it resulted in not *one* board member being placed on a nonprofit board?"

"Goose eggs. Zero," Peter replied.

I remember thinking to myself in that moment: *Well, I know I can do better than that.* So, this time I decided to go rogue, applying for and receiving a grant to design, build, and launch a pilot board placement program for young professionals. I was soon able to convince three well-known companies to join us, inviting their thirty-something professionals to find a board seat through our work. Within a year, we had facilitated the election of more than one hundred professionals to nonprofit governing boards in New York City, Chicago, San Francisco, Los Angeles, and Washington DC.

But a year later, as I suspected, it was decided by the Taproot board of directors that the pilot board placement program was outside of Taproot's core mission. I made my case to the board of directors at a board retreat in Los Angeles, but in the end, they decided to pull the plug. I was heartbroken. Not only had I found my passion, but the program that my team and I had built was working as well.

I understood the board's reasoning, to be sure, but hated to see this successful pilot die on the vine.

A couple weeks later, I visited Peter Sloane to share with him that the program wouldn't continue. Surprised, he asked, "Why? The pilot has been a big success!" Peter's disappointment and frustration were matched by my own. I could think of nothing I would enjoy doing more than facilitating the matching of talented professionals to nonprofit board service opportunities across the country, helping hundreds—or, dare I dream, thousands or even tens of thousands—of professionals find and serve their cause. Even so, the board had made their decision, and the program wasn't going to continue at Taproot.

About a week later, I was walking down Fifth Avenue to a business meeting in Manhattan when I was struck by a thought: *Rob, you love this work. Peter loves it too. We've built an innovative model that is ready to scale, and the Heckscher Foundation wants to fund it.* So, in a moment of courage, I took my cell phone out of my pocket and called Peter Sloane.

"Peter, I have a crazy idea that I'd like to share with you," I managed to squeak out after he picked up.

"I can't talk right now, Rob. I'm on my way out the door for a vacation. Call me back in a week."

I decided I couldn't wait. That evening, I sat at the dinner table and typed out a detailed proposal to the Heckscher Foundation for Children. I described what I would do if provided a grant from the foundation's capacity building and technical assistance fund to begin this work in earnest. I guaranteed that I would find at least three companies to partner in the effort and that I would place scores of professionals on nonprofit boards in the first year. I didn't know the *who* or the *how*, but I knew the *what* and the *why*. Around midnight, I emailed the proposal to Peter.

A week later, while vacationing in Barcelona, a notification flashed on my cell phone screen. Peter had replied. As I shakily clicked into my email account, I pulled up his response. It had just three words: "We are in."

I read and reread the three words over and over again. "We are in." Was I truly contemplating quitting my job to go it alone? No salary. No benefits. No team. No board. No office. And as a lifelong nonprofit professional, I had just a few thousand dollars in my bank account. Would I be able to summon the courage to make a choice as risky as this?

I had a life-crossroad decision to make and about twenty-four hours to decide.

Barcelona

Tourists find an assortment of things when visiting Barcelona. Some come across architectural wonders like Antoni Gaudí's Sagrada Família or Park Güell. Others discover beautiful Mediterranean beaches and world-class museums. Still others will find new culinary delights through the city's tapas culture.

Well, when I was in Barcelona, I found my calling.

There I was, standing alone in the historic Gothic Quarter, staring at my phone, with a course-altering life decision to make. Accept Peter Sloane's offer, quit my job, and venture out on my own? Or play it safe, decline the opportunity, and continue along the career path that had served me well.

In pivotal moments of decision-making like this, I don't know about you, but I need to have a conversation with God. Conveniently, the Catedral de Barcelona was just a short walk away. The Gothic cathedral's construction began in the late thirteenth century. Standing majestically for over seven centuries, its light-brown stone facade is magnificent, with soaring spires directing one's eyes toward the heavens. The cathedral's interior is no less awe inspiring with ornate pillars, vaulted ceilings, and stunning stained glass windows, combined with a rather dark, imposing, and almost heavy atmosphere. As I sat in the cathedral that afternoon, its blend of uplifting transcendence and profound weightiness matched the moment I was in.

For some time, I settled quietly into the pew—calming my mind, thinking about the decision, praying, and looking for a sense of divine inspiration. Some of this time was spent thinking through very practical questions: *What risks are involved? What will be my Plan B if I don't succeed? How soon might money run out? What companies will agree to do this with me? Is my idea even a good one in the first place?*

Other questions were more esoteric: *What does it mean to trust God in a moment like this? Do I have the courage to make a leap of faith of this magnitude?* As I reflect on that moment, I was really asking God one simple question: *If I do this, will you have my back?*

I knew that creating a company from the ground up wouldn't be easy, but I was also clear about three things that ultimately helped me find the courage to take the leap.

1. I felt like I had a good idea to build on.

2. I had established connections with people who were in positions at target companies to buy what I would be selling.

3. I trusted my work ethic. I was prepared to work my tail off. I knew I couldn't guarantee success, but I *could* guarantee that I would do everything in my power to make it work.

About an hour later, I walked out of the Barcelona Cathedral with a strong sense of clarity and peace. I took my cell phone out of my pocket and wrote a reply email to Peter: "Your confidence in this idea and me personally means the world." When I pushed send, for better or worse, there was no doubt that my life had changed forever. With that email, Cause Strategy Partners was born.

So, that's my story. That's how I found my life's work and one of my primary causes.

Now, let's get to the most important business at hand—finding yours.

Chapter Two

Taking the First Step: Finding Your Cause

The place God calls you to is the place where your deep gladness and the world's deep hunger meet.

—FREDERICK BUECHNER,
Wishful Thinking: A Seeker's ABC

Years ago, the organization I was leading, CGLA, needed to sell its building. Positioned near the corner of Division and Wells in the City of Chicago, our staff size had outgrown the office space that served the organization well for many years. The unremarkable, two-story, box-like brick building had been purchased by the organization in 1986 for $210,000 when the neighborhood was dominated by the Cabrini-Green Homes, a notorious public housing development on the Near North Side of Chicago. The process of demolishing the Cabrini-Green public housing units began in 1995 and was completed in 2011, marking the completion of a redevelopment plan for the neighborhood. Our organization's location, once squarely rooted in Cabrini-Green, was now considered part of the highly desirable Old Town neighborhood. There was no doubt that the property's value had increased exponentially as the community around it changed, but by how much?

In order to inform the process of selling the building, we arranged for the Illinois Facilities Fund—a lending, development, and real estate consulting firm—to conduct an appraisal of the building's value. To my surprise, the final report concluded that "the highest and best use" of the property would be to demolish the building entirely and build something new on the land it occupied. I didn't see that coming. The "highest and best use" of the building, it turned out, would be to turn it into no building at all.

The Highest and Best Use

I've often thought about that phrase—"the highest and best use"—as it relates to the use of time. For busy professionals like you, living full lives, time is your most precious resource, and there's never enough of it.

Maybe you commute to an office each day, work full-time, and then commute home. Perhaps you care for rambunctious kids, a legion of plants, a high-maintenance pet, or an aging parent. You likely maintain a home and try to maintain your physical well-being, as well, with an exercise regimen. Perhaps you try to hit the town with your spouse or partner from time to time, hoping to have some semblance of a social life. Then there are the mundane tasks of daily life: shopping for groceries, preparing meals, and doing laundry. You occasionally need to visit the doctor, the dentist, and your barber or beautician. You reserve time on weekends to run errands. Maybe you spend an hour on Saturdays at Home Depot or Target with a few hundred of your closest friends. You'd like to find time for a family getaway, but just planning the vacation seems impossible to get to on your to-do list.

Given the full set of demands you face every day, it's critical that you find and focus on the cause that will matter most to you. There's a limited supply of time, and none of us knows just how finite our own supply may be. "Lost time," as Benjamin Franklin wrote, "is never found again." So in the spirit of getting "the highest and best use" out of the time you invest in service to your community, state, nation, or the world, let's begin to uncover your unique, distinctive, personal cause.

Ten Questions to Uncover Your Cause

My friend, Brandon Freeman, and I are in an article club together with a small group of friends. (It's like a book club, but we're too busy to commit to reading books at the same pace, so we read and discuss articles instead.) One evening, as the six of us sat in my living room discussing the topic of the moment, Brandon said, "I really don't have a passion for a cause at all. I think the idea of having a passion for something is sort of odd to begin with." Now, you have to understand that Brandon is brilliant with a wealth of talent to offer the world. He's a lawyer, a finance expert, one of the most well-read people I know, a traveler, inquisitive, and works at a prominent tech company. In other words, Brandon is an easy mark for a guy like me who spends his life connecting talented professionals to their purpose.

For weeks I couldn't get Brandon's comments out of my mind, so I eventually decided to try to explore with him where his passion for serving a cause might lie. Sometime earlier, I'd written a set of questions designed to help a person uncover their cause area. This was the perfect opportunity to give these questions a test run.

I sent Brandon an email: "I'm wondering if you'd be willing to take a few minutes to respond to some quick questions I've developed to help professionals who may not have a clear sense of what their 'cause' is in an effort to move from uncertainty to clarity." In the true spirit of a time-strapped attorney, Brandon wrote back quickly in a two-sentence email: "Would love to help on this. I'll set aside some time this weekend so I can give some thoughtful answers." And late one evening about a week later, he did.

As Brandon worked through the questions, he began to identify social challenges that resonated with him: the burden of student loan debt on young people, the lack of affordable housing, cancer patients being strapped with exorbitant medical bills, and helping young people get access to a quality higher education. He also described examples of being moved when he witnessed random acts of kindness between strangers.

In addition to identifying a handful of specific causes, the exercise clarified for Brandon that he's more drawn to helping individuals directly than supporting organizations that address societal challenges on a structural level. It turns out Brandon had more cause area interests than he realized at first blush.

Whatever your starting point may be—whether you're already a Causie with more interests than you know what to do with, or you're new to thinking about this altogether—I want to encourage you to reflect on these same ten questions. Give yourself fifteen minutes to process them and jot down your answers on the following pages.

1. What important life experiences shaped you during your childhood?

2. What is your personal value system? Who or what played a leading role in helping you develop it?

3. What are your hobbies? What activities fill you with contentment, joy, or even exhilaration?

4. What substantial challenge has impacted your life or the life of a loved one?

5. What has been a precious gift you received in life that many others aren't as fortunate to have enjoyed?

6. When was the last time you welled up with emotion about a circumstance unrelated to your own life? What was it that moved you?

7. Observe your reaction to news headlines. What events evoke strong emotions within you? What two or three social issues do you find yourself talking about most often with family and friends?

8. When you think about the future, what societal condition causes you the most concern?

9. As you walk around your neighborhood or drive around your city, what do you see that frustrates you? Conversely, what do you see that inspires you?

10. What could you talk about for twenty uninterrupted minutes?

Homing in on Your Cause

These questions are designed to get the mental wheels turning on two areas of inquiry fundamental to identifying your cause: (1) What societal need resonates with you? and (2) What are you passionate about?

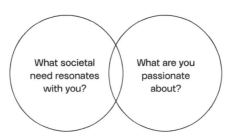

WHAT SOCIETAL NEED RESONATES WITH YOU?

I realize that bringing up the U.S. Internal Revenue Service—affectionately known as the "IRS"—is a sure way to get you to quit this book or use it as a sleep aid to help you doze off. But do me a favor and stick with me for a moment because this is important.

The IRS has established several classifications for tax-exempt organizations, including:

- charitable organizations such as those that focus on religion, education, healthcare, science and research, arts and culture, the environment, and social services, to name a few;

- social welfare organizations that promote the common good and general welfare of the community;

- business-oriented organizations that promote the common interests of members;

- societies and associations that provide benefits to members; and

- veterans' organizations that operate exclusively for those who have served in the military.

Now, to go one step further, the National Taxonomy of Exempt Entities (NTEE) is a coding system developed by the National Center for Charitable Statistics to provide a standardized way of describing the activities of various nonprofit entities. (Think the Dewey Decimal system, but for nonprofits rather than books.) The NTEE classifies nonprofit organizations based on their primary mission or purpose.

> **There are more than 650 unique types of charitable organizations. Your challenge won't be in finding a societal problem, need, or opportunity that could use your help.**

Care to guess how many categories the NTEE has identified to classify the various types of nonprofits? The answer is pretty astounding; there are more than 650 unique types of charitable organizations. Your challenge won't be in finding a societal problem, need, or opportunity that could use your help. There are literally hundreds and hundreds of causes. They are all around you. Consider this high-level list of the types of organizations doing social good in our society, as categorized by the NTEE:

- Arts, Culture, and Humanities
- Education
- Environment
- Animal-Related
- Healthcare
- Mental Health and Crisis Intervention

- Voluntary Health Associations and Medical Disciplines
- Medical Research
- Crime and Legal-Related
- Employment
- Food, Agriculture, and Nutrition
- Housing and Shelter
- Public Safety, Disaster Preparedness, and Relief
- Recreation and Sports
- Youth Development
- Human Services
- International, Foreign Affairs, and National Security
- Civil Rights, Social Action, and Advocacy
- Philanthropy, Volunteerism, and Grantmaking Foundations
- Science and Technology
- Social Science
- Public and Societal Benefit
- Religion-Related
- Mutual and Membership Benefit

Review this list and circle two or three categories that seem to map most closely with your responses to the Ten Questions to Uncover Your Cause. By narrowing down the categories in this way, you'll be starting to land on your answer to the question, "What societal need resonates with you?"

WHAT ARE YOU PASSIONATE ABOUT?

While my friend Brandon initially reacted somewhat skeptically to the idea of having a "passion," it became clear that he had a few after working through the ten questions. I especially appreciated this response: "My sister got very sick and we were all wondering how her treatment would be paid for since she had no health insurance. It turns out there's some kind of nonprofit that sponsors certain types of cancer patients and they agreed to take care of all of her medical bills. I'm sure this played a huge role in her emotional state during treatment. It was amazing to see that these types of organizations exist."

Brandon also reflected on how he is moved by random acts of kindness, writing: "The only time I can authentically say that I have an emotional response is when I see someone acting very kindly—for example, an elderly lady on the bus last week struck up a conversation with some young girls and showed them genuine care. She gave them some old lady pearls of wisdom. Or when someone lets you pass first on the street and gives you a big smile. Or anytime you see someone being kinder than they need to be."

Reflecting on Brandon's responses, his cause area might focus in on mentorship, intergenerational connectiveness, the provision of no-cost healthcare, or championing civility and kindness in society. There are plenty of organizations working in each one of these areas, but we'll save that—finding an organizational home for your cause—for the next chapter.

As you review your responses to the ten questions, what personal passions jump off the page? When I went through this exercise, a number of my passion themes emerged, including diversity and inclusion, musical theater and the performing arts, second chances for formerly incarcerated individuals, camping, and educational equity. What comes up for you?

Head Passion and Heart Passion

When I'm working with professionals who are in the process of exploring their cause area, I like to remind them to expand their definition of passion beyond the heart. Passion is, of course, intrinsically linked to emotion. That's a good starting point. But there are other causes and organizations that could better be described as matters of the head rather than the heart.

In 2014, my colleagues Allie Hallock, Kate Effland, Alanya Green, and I traveled to Atlanta, Georgia, to interview board chairs and CEOs of nonprofit organizations that had applied for our pilot board placement program. Each forty-five-minute interview provided the opportunity for these nonprofit leaders to pitch their organization, shining a light on the mission, vision, values, and programs behind the organization's work. Nonprofit leaders are passionate folks: it's always inspiring to hear them talk about the importance of the service their organization is doing for the community.

One organization we met with spoke directly to our hearts. The mission of New American Pathways is to help refugees, and the state of Georgia, thrive. Their vision is "for new Americans in metro Atlanta to become successful, contributing, and welcomed members of Georgia's communities" by offering a comprehensive continuum of services from arrival through citizenship. Their stories of success are stirring, describing how New American Pathways helped vulnerable families fleeing war and other dangers find shelter in the United States and then learn the English language, secure employment, navigate the complexities of the healthcare system, apply for citizenship, and purchase homes. By the end of their interview, we were moved and inspired.

Shortly thereafter, we interviewed the leaders of the Atlanta Community ToolBank, which provides year-round access to tools and other costly equipment through a lending program for nonprofits serving the Atlanta region. Their motto? "Lending tools is our thing. Our services help organizations do their thing." In 2022, the ToolBank fulfilled 749 orders for 182 member nonprofits, saving these agencies $2.5 million dollars in purchased tools so that those monies could be reinvested in programs and services to serve the Atlanta community. That, my friend, is a smart idea.

Even so, I worried aloud with my colleagues that we wouldn't find candidates interested in serving on the Atlanta Community ToolBank board. "Where was the emotional hook?" I wondered. "Would people get excited about this mission? After all, they don't have moving life stories of program success." Boy, was I wrong! In fact, the ToolBank ended up being the most requested nonprofit by our board candidates in the program's round. The ToolBank appeals to the head rather than the heart. It's a brilliant idea and a great solution for a specific challenge faced by Atlanta's social good community.

Are you a Heart Passion person? Will you need to have an emotional connection to the work that will serve as an ongoing source of inspiration and motivation? Or is it more important that you connect to a really smart, compelling, innovative idea? If so, Head Passion may be at the center of what you're looking for.

Getting Closer: Two More Questions

By this point, you are likely close to identifying your cause. You might even think you've landed on it. For good measure, there are two more factors that should be considered in this exploration. Answers to these questions will also be important in matching yourself to an organization, which we'll cover in the next chapter.

1. Is your sweet spot working directly with individuals, or is having a larger societal impact of more importance to you?

2. Do you need to see the immediate impact of your efforts or are you more interested in pursuing lasting, durable change?

INDIVIDUAL IMPACT VERSUS SOCIETAL IMPACT

Direct service involves providing assistance, resources, and support directly to beneficiaries such as clients, families, students, patients, or stray animals, to name a few. Direct service work is hands-on, face-to-face, and centered on the needs of individual clients—on driving impact at the individual level.

Policy and advocacy work, on the other hand, focuses on the macro level in order to effect positive structural change. These efforts tend to center on research, awareness raising, mobilizing the public's support, and advocating for changes to the law. Policy and advocacy work seeks systemic change and enduring impact for the many rather than the individual.

An animal lover, for example, might find their cause in caring for our four-legged furry friends. We all have these people in our lives, don't we? Their social media is full of pictures of cats and dogs. The idea of a stray animal roaming the streets—hungry, injured, vulnerable to predation and disease—keeps them up at night. They absolutely will not go see a film featuring a dog that dies in the end.

There are two very different ways an animal lover might go about serving their cause. In direct services, the work might focus on rescuing strays, providing medical treatment, and finding them a permanent home. These Causies might volunteer on weekends at the local shelter, socializing with and walking dogs as they wait for an adopted home. They are likely to provide financial resources to no-kill shelters and may drop goody bags off from time to time full of treats, chewable toys, or comfort towels.

There are also ways to help animals that don't involve coming into contact with them at all. Animal advocacy groups, for example, work to pass laws ending dog racing and restricting the breeding or sale of certain animals. You're more likely to find these Causies raising awareness about the use of animals in scientific experiments, making donations to wildlife conservation projects, protesting an unethical breeding facility, or distributing consumer education research on factory farming practices.

Which style resonates most with you? Something direct where you can experience the benefit of your service firsthand as you drive positive impact? Or something more systemic in nature that aims to get to the root of a problem, creating positive solutions for society as a whole?

IMMEDIATE VERSUS LONG-TERM IMPACT

Think also about your tolerance for the pace of change. Some of us weren't gifted with patience, after all. Count me high on that list. We never stand on a moving sidewalk at the airport, for example. You'll find us walking briskly in the left lane, annoyed with the people standing in our way. We won't wait for an ice-cream cone after dinner if the line is longer than two people. Throughout the workday, we find great satisfaction in crossing things off our to-do list. Such individuals might be inclined to focus on causes that have an immediate impact and address pressing needs with a specific action.

Others will view those types of efforts as a poor use of their valuable time and resources, opting instead to focus on lasting, sustainable, long-term solutions. While they may not see firsthand the fruits of their efforts, they know they're making an investment in the future, addressing underlying issues and systemic challenges rather than reflexively responding to urgent needs.

Wendy spent the first decade of her life in the foster care system and was fortunate enough to get adopted through a foster-to-adopt program when she turned eleven. Almost all of her friends from when she was younger "aged out" of the system at eighteen, largely left to fend for themselves. Many didn't fare well.

Wendy has a huge heart for foster care children and wanted to do something to make a difference in their lives. Somewhat surprisingly, however, she passed on an opportunity to mentor emancipated foster youth. Instead, she joined a recently formed organization developing a distributed housing model and offering self-sufficiency training for emancipated foster youth. As a start-up, the nonprofit wouldn't begin serving young people for more than a year, and the program design called for participants to engage over an extended period of time in educational programs, workforce readiness, financial literacy, and health and wellness activities. Wendy wouldn't likely see the fruit of her labor for many years, but she was convinced that over the long term, she would be able to support more youth by helping the budding organization find its footing. She liked the idea of a holistic program with its many components aiming for lasting change.

Where do you fall on this continuum? Is seeing the beneficial effect of your work right away of high importance to you? Or is it more important that you invest your personal resources in initiatives focused on having a long-term positive impact?

Let's Identify Your Causie Style!

By assessing where you land on these two continuums, you will be closer to understanding the cause area that is right for you. In the following two-by-two table, mark an "X" in the quadrant that most closely reflects your personal style. If you lean toward causes that help the individual rather than seek societal solutions, for example, your mark belongs somewhere below the horizontal line. If systemic impact is more important to you, your "X" will show up in the upper half of the chart. Similarly, if you want to see more immediate impact as a result of your efforts, your mark belongs on the left side of the table, but if driving long-term impact is your priority, your mark will show up on the right side of the vertical line. Having identified where you land on this graph helps you understand an important part of your Causie profile. Are you a Helping Hand, a Disruptor, a Reformer, or a People Developer?

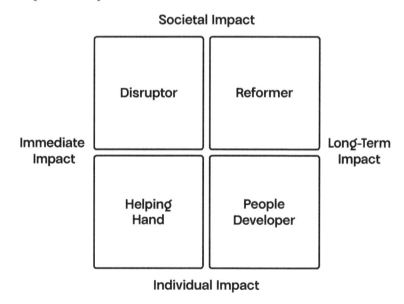

Helping Hands are intrinsically motivated by a desire to alleviate suffering, solve problems, and make a positive impact in the individual lives of others. Their North Star is to provide direct, immediate support to others in need, and they're not afraid to roll up their sleeves. This might manifest through work with organizations that offer guidance, resources, or practical help to individuals, families, or groups facing various challenges. Helping Hands might be drawn, for instance, to organizations focused on delivering emergency aid, disaster relief, humanitarian support, and other forms of on-the-ground assistance to those in need.

People Developers are driven by a desire to help others achieve their full potential. They seek to empower others, helping them to grow and develop over the long term. These Causies work toward creating permanent, sustainable impact in the lives of the people they work with, embodying the idea that if you can make a difference for one person, it's worth the effort. As such, People Developers might be drawn to organizations that provide ongoing services to individuals, such as mentorship programs, workforce development, or coaching to help others build skills, confidence, and self-awareness.

Reformers seek to address problems in our society by building on or modifying existing systems and structures. They strive for societal-level impact and are willing to be patient, working to improve our present world over time in order to achieve more fundamental, lasting change that will benefit future generations. Reformers might be drawn to organizations that challenge the status quo by engaging with policy, advocacy, research, and legal issues across a wide range of cause areas, working to establish policies and practices conducive to a more just society.

Disruptors seek to upend the status quo and create change by challenging existing systems or structures. These Causies aren't afraid to operate outside of established institutions, and they're open to unconventional or even controversial methods to achieve their goals.

Disruptors are focused on rapid change, often prioritizing innovation and experimentation over tradition and stability. Disruptors might be drawn to organizations working on the cutting edge of the cause areas they engage with, such as those leveraging novel applications of technology, testing innovative business models, finding unique ways to connect under-resourced communities with opportunities, and forging new types of partnerships to advance their mission.

Identify Your Style Online with MyCauseFinder.com

Cause Strategy Partners has developed MyCauseFinder.com, an online assessment tool designed to assist users in identifying their distinct approach to driving social impact. After responding to a series of questions, users will receive a personalized Causie profile to assist them in discovering their cause and identifying the ideal type of nonprofit organization for engagement. As you round out this first step in your Causie journey, consider taking fifteen minutes right now to complete the MyCauseFinder.com questions and discover your Causie style.

What's Next?

After you identify the cause area you're meant to serve, the next step is to find it an organizational home. As my colleague Ashley Bratrud describes it, "[A]fter the inner work comes the outer work of finding an organization." The next chapter will show you how.

Reflection Questions

1. Do you expect to be drawn to causes that appeal primarily to the head or to the heart? Do you need to feel the impact of the work? Or is a really smart idea more important to you?

2. What is your Causie profile? Are you a Helping Hand, a People Developer, a Reformer, or a Disruptor?

3. Let's put it all together and try to define your cause right now before we move on. If you're stuck, consider using MyCauseFinder.com to help you get clarity. Use the following space to write it down.

MY CAUSE IS ...

Chapter
Three

Identifying the Right Organization for You

Alone we can do so little. Together we can do so much.

—HELEN KELLER

My firm, Cause Strategy Partners, has connected thousands of professionals to nonprofit board service opportunities through our signature program, BoardLead. It's truly inspiring to watch the individuals we partner with identify a nonprofit at the center of their personal passion and then go on to serve and support the organization's work. As each one engages with their nonprofit, we witness them catalyze tangible change on a cause area close to their heart.

One leader we were honored to partner with is a powerful example of what can happen when someone finds the perfect organization for them to serve. Carl Gaines moved to New York City as a young man in 1998. He had recently learned that he was HIV positive and, like many LGBTQ+ people from small towns, wanted to be in a large city where he could feel safe and find community with others who had similar life experiences. Carl understood the risk he was taking relocating from Charlottesville, Virginia, to New York City.

"There are two things in life," Carl explained, "that are critical for people to be safe and have the chance for a stable life: The first is healthcare and the second is housing. Without both of these in place, it's really difficult to get a foothold, especially in a city like New York, which will spit you right back out pretty quickly." Carl had a place to stay when he arrived in the city, but he had no healthcare and was particularly vulnerable given his HIV diagnosis. He was soon told about Callen-Lorde, a leading healthcare center in New York specializing in comprehensive services for the LGBTQ+ community, as well as those living with HIV/AIDS. He learned that Callen-Lorde provided high-quality care regardless of a patient's ability to pay. Carl became a patient at Callen-Lorde in no time. "Having that aspect of my life taken care of allowed me to not only stay in New York City, but also enabled me to build a career, a social network, and eventually become a successful New Yorker."

Many years later, in 2018, Carl was working as a senior manager at a financial services firm that was partnering with BoardLead to place their executives and employees on nonprofit boards. Carl heard about the opportunity from his colleague and enthusiastically applied. As a part of the process, Carl reviewed a number of one-page profiles of BoardLead nonprofit partners. "When I came across Callen-Lorde," Carl shared with me, "I stopped looking further. I was so excited. Here was an organization I was perfectly aligned with from a mission standpoint that had also been my healthcare provider for more than a decade."

After BoardLead made the match, Carl moved through Callen-Lorde's vetting and nomination process and was elected to the board of directors in just a few months. He has been able to make a significant impact on the work of the organization, a global leader in LGBTQ+ healthcare, while leveraging his unique perspective as both a patient and a board member. Carl has since been elected to an officer role by his fellow board members, growing his leadership responsibilities at the organization.

Despite receiving private healthcare insurance through his employer, which, of course, opens up access to a range of healthcare providers, Carl won't go anywhere else for his healthcare needs. "The Callen-Lorde staff is so hard working," he explains. "I know this because I've seen it for years. I have direct insight into what it's like sitting in the waiting room, watching the staff care for patients without judgment even though many can't pay, always putting patient dignity first. I'm a better patient and a better board member as a result of being involved with the organization on multiple levels. At the end of the day, providing healthcare to people who are marginalized and don't have access to it is what we at Callen-Lorde care so deeply about."

Carl found his organization. Now let's find yours.

Finding Your Cause a Home

Now that you've defined your cause area, it's time to find it an organizational home. Given the demands on your time, you'll want to optimize your impact by connecting in meaningful ways to a nonprofit organization that will provide you with the very best opportunity to make a lasting impact on your cause. This should be an organization you believe in, trust, find inspiration from, and are excited to support. And once you find that perfect organization, there remains the challenge of connecting with the nonprofit, the leadership, and its team members who are doing the work.

With 1.8 million nonprofit organizations in the United States, 185,000 charities in the United Kingdom, and approximately ten million nongovernmental organizations worldwide,[2] finding that one right organization for you may sound like a daunting task. The following six best practices will arm you with strategies to help you get it right.

START CLOSE TO HOME WHILE REMAINING OPEN TO MORE DISTANT OPPORTUNITIES

Look around. You might already be involved with a nonprofit organization that serves you: your family's house of worship, the recreation center where you exercise, your children's charter school or afterschool program, your parents' senior center, your local chamber of commerce, or the community theater you subscribe to as a season ticket holder, for example. Your engagement with these organizations has already demonstrated your resonance with their missions. Is there one you'd like to support even more by elevating your involvement? Circumstances couldn't have been better for Carl Gaines. When he discovered that Callen-Lorde was looking for board members, he couldn't raise his hand fast enough.

When you live and work close to an organization's physical location, you can demonstrate your commitment to its mission in tangible ways—by readily serving as a volunteer, attending organizational events, supporting fundraising efforts, and more. If your goal is to secure a board role in the future, starting local is a particularly strategic approach as it allows you to be visible to the staff and leadership, including board members. By showing initiative and being present, you become known to the decision-makers, building rapport

---

2   "15 Interesting nonprofit organizations statistics and facts," TeamStage, accessed March 26, 2024, https://teamstage.io/nonprofit-organizations-statistics/#:~:text=While%20the%20US%20has%20the,UK%20don%27t%20lag%20behind.

and trust. As leadership opportunities develop, you'll already be a known quantity, which is a great place to start.

A second benefit of starting close to home is that you'll have a built-in base of support among your friends, colleagues, and neighbors. Board members who generate resources for an organization from within their network often find it easier to do so when the "ask" is to members of the same community that the organization serves. They rightly see it as neighbor-helping-neighbor when supporting organizations in their own backyard.

It should be noted, however, that in the same way remote work has become more commonplace in society, so too has remote board service. This change is powered by the availability of new technologies as well as shifting mindsets after the pandemic that began in early 2020. In our work through BoardLead, upward of 65 percent of our nonprofit partners now express interest in meeting board candidates who live and work outside of their immediate metropolitan area. Nonprofit leaders increasingly recognize that candidates are well positioned to fulfill most, if not all, board responsibilities remotely.

This increasing openness to remote board service has resulted in both benefits and challenges for nonprofit organizations. On the positive side, it creates a tremendous opportunity for nonprofits to address any number of diversity gaps on their board when the potential candidate pool is as expansive as the country itself. Virtual meetings can also increase board member attendance by eliminating long commute times or making it possible to participate virtually, even when a board member is traveling. This approach offers convenience, flexibility, and the ability to record sessions for those who miss a meeting. More "voices" are often heard in meetings, as well, as the chat box function provides opportunities for dynamic opining even while others are talking.

There are downsides, as well. The most significant, in my view, is that the lack of regular in-person interaction makes it more difficult to develop into a team, build trusting relationships, and engage effectively in complex or difficult conversations. Reliable internet connectivity and adequate technology can also be a challenge as the phrase, "Can you hear me now?" becomes even more prominent in our daily lives.

ENGAGE YOUR NETWORK

In the same way a job seeker alerts people in their network that they are in the market for a new employment opportunity, you should make your interest in serving your cause known among those who are well connected in your world. Set up informational interviews with your friends who are staff members, volunteers, or board members at organizations that interest you. Leverage LinkedIn to discover who in your network has existing connections to board members at interesting organizations. If your employer has a corporate social responsibility or employee engagement team, ask them if the company has a relationship with any nonprofits working in your cause area. These in-house teams are always eager to meet employees interested in participating in the community impact work of the company.

Use social media in this process, as well. Consider messaging your interest on LinkedIn or another platform. Name your cause area, and share that you're interested in ramping up your support. A simple post that says, "Do you know any organization having a positive impact on this issue? All introductions welcome!" could result in a number of strong leads.

CONDUCT AN ONLINE SEARCH

If it turns out that your network isn't rich with individuals supporting nonprofits in your cause area, there's still plenty you can do to find an organization that is a strong match for you. A keyword search on your browser will likely yield several organizations working in your cause area. Depending on the geographic reach you'd like to focus on, keep in mind that you'll likely want to narrow the search by location, as well.

DO YOUR DUE DILIGENCE

After you've found one or more target organizations, it's time to put some research into making sure they pass your due diligence test. At this stage of your search, there are four primary things you will want to consider about the organizations on your short list.

- *Do you believe wholeheartedly in the organization's work?* Nonprofits spend hours in the process of crafting the organization's mission, vision, and values statements. Every word is there for a reason. Do these core messages compel you to learn more about the people, the beneficiaries served, and the overall impact of the work? Does the organization's suite of programs and services appear to be a strategic approach to getting closer to the world they imagine in their long-range vision?

- *Do you sense a strong culture fit with your personal value system?* Visit each organization's website, and pay attention to how it makes you feel. Review the social media profiles of the organizations on your short list, as well. Which organizations have an online presence that fills you with inspiration? Do you sense a strong alignment with your core values?

- *Is leadership compelling and strong?* Now do some sleuthing on the background of the people leading the work, especially the chief executive (often titled the executive director), the board chair, and the organization's board members. Check out their professional bios on the organization's website as well as their LinkedIn profiles. Does the chief executive regularly post inspiring stories about the organization they lead? Does it feel like they view their role as "more than a job" based on their social media presence? Do they appear to be a sector leader or thought leader in the social impact space? What about the board members? Collectively, do they appear to have the requisite experience, diversity, and gravitas to lead the organization effectively? Individually, do they communicate personal passion for the work? For example, have board members made their involvement a part of their personal and professional identity by adding their board service to their professional bio and LinkedIn profile?

- *What rating do nonprofit assessment agencies give the organization?* You're not on your own when it comes to trying to determine if an organization is responsible and well-run in serving their cause. There are professional organizations that do just that, and part of your due diligence is to use these valuable, free services. Start with charitynavigator.org. Where does your organization rate on the well-regarded Charity Navigator scale of zero to four stars? A high rating indicates strong levels of effectiveness, transparency, accountability, financial health, and responsible practices. Cross-reference this report at guidestar.org, which rates a nonprofit's level of transparency. Does your organization receive a Platinum,

Gold, Silver, or Bronze Seal of Transparency? In the social good sector, transparency is a value of tremendous importance.

NOW, GO DEEP: REVIEW THE FORM 990

As you begin to home in on your top priority organization, there is one final step I strongly recommend: review the nonprofit's most recent publicly available Form 990, also known as the Return of Organization Exempt from Income Tax. This annual filing is required by the IRS for most tax-exempt organizations. There are limited exceptions to the filing requirement for certain religious organizations like churches, synagogues, or mosques, as well as very small nonprofits, but the majority of groups you discover will have past filings available online for your review.

To find your target nonprofit's most recently available filing, type "Candid Form 990" into an internet browser, and you will link to a wonderful resource provided by Candid, their 990 Finder. After typing in the nonprofit's name, you'll be able to navigate to the organization's most recently available Form 990.

Now, I'll give you fair warning, there is a *lot* of very detailed information, including countless numbers, on this comprehensive filing. Don't be off put, even if math wasn't your strong suit in school. For the most curious and earnest among us, a full review of the Form 990 will be a treat. For the rest of us, however, we will want to jump straight to the information that can help us make an informed decision as we consider whether to support and engage with our target organization's work.

What should you focus on when conducting due diligence for the organization you're interested in potentially supporting? I suggest investigating the following thirteen items in their Form 990 (see the Appendix):

1. *What year was the organization formed?* Is this a start-up, developing, mature, or storied organization? *Box L at the top of the form, page 1*

2. *How large is the team?* How many board members, employees, and volunteers support the work? *Part I summary, page 1*

3. *What was the size of the organization's annual revenue? Part I, row 12*

4. *How much did they spend that fiscal year? Part I, row 18*

5. *Did they finish the fiscal year with a surplus or deficit? Part I, row 19*

6. *What are the net assets or fund balances of the organization?* Are cash reserves sufficient to support a financially stable future? *Part I, row 22*

7. *Did the organization's finances grow or shrink over the last two years? Compare "Prior Year" to "Current Year" columns*

8. *What are the largest programs the organization invests in and what outcomes did each one achieve? Part III, section 4*

9. *Who are the board members?* Did they receive compensation for their service? Keep in mind that employees serving on the board almost always receive compensation (e.g., the executive director), but in most cases, payment is generally viewed as inappropriate for nonemployee board members in the nonprofit sector. *Part VII, section A*

10. *What is the chief executive's compensation, as well as other highly compensated employees?* Does their compensation seem appropriate given the size of the organization and the skill set required to perform the role effectively? *The specific section*

where this information is reported varies, but you should be able to find it with a close look, including Part VII, section A and Schedule J.

11. *How much did the organization spend on program services as compared to management and fundraising expenses?* Does the organization appear to be prioritizing programmatic impact in its spending? *Part IX, row 25*

12. *For those who are particularly savvy in financial management, consider whether the balance sheet looks healthy. Part X*

13. *Spend a few minutes with the schedules at the end of the Form 990.* Often the schedules contain insightful information that isn't presented earlier.

If you end up serving on an organization's governing board, keep in mind that your name will be listed on the IRS Form 990, as well. For that reason alone, it's important that board members review the Form 990 before it's filed, know its contents, and understand the information that will be available to the public about the organization and its work.

IF DUE DILIGENCE RESULTS IN AN "ALL-CLEAR," IT'S TIME TO MAKE YOURSELF KNOWN

A nonprofit executive director once told me about an interesting phone call she received. A gentleman she'd never met introduced himself, sharing lots of information about his background with a healthy dose of ego mixed in. He wrapped up with a request: "I'd like to be considered for your board." After politely engaging in the conversation and hanging up the phone, this executive director walked down the hallway to her director of development's office. She asked her chief fundraiser if the caller had previously made a donation to support the organization's work. Searching the donor database, the answer came back, "Nope, no contribution on record."

The executive director then stopped by the office of the volunteer coordinator to see if the caller had ever served as a volunteer. Again, after searching through the database, no prior contact was found. Finally, she asked the organization's receptionist if she'd heard of the individual or had any recollection of him visiting the program. Again, the answer was "no." The gentleman's first known contact with the organization, it turns out, was a rather brazen request to be granted a leadership role as a member of the board.

That, friend, is exactly what *not* to do. Lead with generosity, humility, and curiosity as you make yourself known to an organization that interests you. While the gentleman described made the mistake of coming in too hot, you also don't want to make the mistake of doing nothing at all. Becoming a Causie is an intentional decision to get involved. The good news is that there is a range of escalating ways to engage with a nonprofit. You don't need to accelerate from zero to sixty in a week, a month, or even a year. But *do* get started.

This chart outlines several roles that you can take on as a champion for an organization working in your cause area. Each role demonstrates your commitment to the mission. Each action shows the organization that you're eager to be a part of supporting the work. And each one requires varying degrees of time commitment and expertise to get the job done. If you're new to an organization, working your way down the chart—from ambassador to donor, from volunteer to fundraiser, from advisor or pro bono consultant to the governing board—is a wonderfully organic way to make yourself known.

ROLE	ACTION	TIME REQUIRED	EXPERTISE REQUIRED	EXAMPLE
Ambassador	Raise awareness about the organization's work within your network.	Low	Low	Share social media postings from the organization.
Donor	Make a financial donation to support the organization's work.	Low	Low	Set up a monthly contribution using the "donate" button on the website.
Volunteer	Contribute time in support of the organization's activities or projects.	Variable, low to high	Variable, generally low	Assist in serving a meal at a shelter.
Fundraiser	Secure financial support for the organization from your network.	Variable, generally low	Variable, low to medium	Host a house party to introduce the organization to your friends and ask for support.
Advisor	Provide ongoing mentorship and advice to leadership.	Medium	Medium to high	Serve on a committee, auxiliary board, or task force.
Pro Bono Consultant	Use your professional skills to support an organizational need, at no cost.	Medium to high	High, in your area of professional expertise	A marketing professional contributes her expertise to build a social media strategy for an upcoming campaign.
Board Member	Govern, shepherd, and support an organization	High	Medium to high, understanding and performing the role of a board member	Serve on the board of directors

Consider how many hours per month you can commit to give the organization. For those unable to carve out much time in support of the organization, the Ambassador and Donor roles are likely the best starting point. For those who can invest a number of hours in support of the mission, explore what volunteer opportunities might exist and whether there's a need for your professional skill set on a pro bono project. Offering to support the organization by fundraising from within your personal network will, most likely, raise your profile very quickly among the organization's leadership. Wherever you land, do something! Taking action is your next step in becoming a Causie.

A Causie Story: Kerri Catalano

I'm not used to having people charge over to me in a crowded room, so when that happened at a Credit Suisse event I'd been invited to—a celebration of service for the company's employees engaged in community service—I was a bit taken aback.

An unfamiliar face popped up in front of me and asked, "Aren't you Rob Acton?"

"I am," I replied, as I quickly scrolled through the visual Rolodex in my brain, trying to place her face.

"I'm Kerri Catalano. I work here at Credit Suisse. I recognize you from the board training you led a while back here at the bank and I really want to tell you my story."

"I'd love to hear it!" I enthusiastically replied.

"I have a twin brother who was bullied in school," Kerri began. "Growing up, I witnessed firsthand the damage that bullying can cause, especially in the middle school years." Kerri went on to explain how Credit Suisse had invited her to apply for a nonprofit board seat through BoardLead. "When I was going through the process,

I reflected a lot on the life experiences that had an impact on me as a kid and I realized a central theme was the bullying that my twin brother faced when we were younger." She decided her board service should focus on changing that reality for young people growing up facing similar situations.

Crystal clear on her cause, Kerri discovered Beyond Differences, a San Francisco-based nonprofit with a mission to "ensure that every child in middle school feels accepted, included and valued by their peers, no matter what their difference." As a New York City resident, joining the board of an organization based in San Francisco would mean an elevated level of commitment for Kerri, with added travel demands and the need for increased intentionality in making connections with fellow board members, staff, and the students the organization serves. Even so, Kerri didn't hesitate—she was all in.

At Credit Suisse that day, Kerri said something that I'll never forget. "Your program, BoardLead, helped me find my purpose. This is what I was meant to do." Since joining the Beyond Differences Board of Directors, Kerri's time has been put to its highest and best use. According to the organization's executive director:

> *Kerri came in like a spark plug and made other people take notice. She rose to vice chair of the board within a matter of months and now makes presentations at pretty much every board meeting. Kerri organized a volunteering event for us at her company. She is relentless in pursuing fundraising grants from big institutions and unafraid of cold-calling and asking other people for support.*

Kerri identified her passion and her cause. She went through a thorough process of uncovering how she wanted to make a difference and discovered an organization where she could bring her purpose to life.

What's Next

Finding an organizational home filled with like-minded individuals dedicated to your cause is deeply satisfying and inspiring. Knowing that there's a place for your "causiness" to flourish is heartwarming. It's the start of a journey that can add meaning and value to your life, not to mention provide you with a group of new friends you already have something in common with.

When you're a Causie, you'll talk passionately about the organization's work with your family, friends, and colleagues. When you're a Causie, you'll raise the profile of the organization within your network in order to generate more and more support. When you're a Causie, you'll continually seek ways to grow your involvement with the organization and the impact it has on your cause.

The deepest level of involvement a professional can have with a nonprofit organization is generally found in serving on the board of directors. If taking on a board leadership role sounds intriguing, the rest of this book will help you understand what it requires, how to earn the role, and what it looks like to make the most of your time as you serve your cause from a seat on a nonprofit organization's board.

Reflections

- What nonprofit organizations are you already involved with? Might one of them be a good place for you to escalate your involvement?

- Which organizations have a mission and online content that resonate most deeply with you?

- Whom should you connect with to share your interest in serving an organization in your cause area?

- What organizations are on your short list as potential homes for your cause? How did they fare in your due diligence exercise?

- Which of the Causie roles is likely to be the right starting point for you? Which one do you aspire to?

Chapter
Four

What Is Nonprofit Board Service?

With great power there must also come great responsibility.

—UNCLE BEN TO PETER PARKER IN *SPIDER-MAN*

"Boards suck. Try to keep the board out of your hair as much as possible."

I was stepping into a new leadership role as a first-time nonprofit chief executive, and this was the initial piece of advice I received from an individual who served in a similar role.

"Boards don't help you out. They slow things down. They don't really understand what's going on in the organization. They're mostly a drag on the work, so my advice is to put as little in front of them as you can."

I've since learned that she wasn't the first nonprofit executive to have that perspective. Over many years serving as a board consultant and governance trainer, I've heard sentiments like these over and over again, articulated in various ways. And I must admit it's not entirely unfair or untrue.

The Truth about Nonprofit Boards

Boards often *do* slow things down. Board members aren't around to fully understand the day-to-day operation of the organization. Boards don't always operate with the strongest foundation of information. Too often, they don't put their best foot forward in governing, shepherding, and supporting the organization's work.

So, then, the question must be asked, "Why does the legal structure require that nonprofits are overseen by boards?" Wouldn't it be much more efficient, for example, if the chief executive of a nonprofit had the same amount of autonomy as does a business entrepreneur? Take Sarah Blakely, the creator of Spanx, the body-shaping undergarments for women. A self-made billionaire, Sarah took no outside investment. She made independent decisions on business strategy, pricing, product development, factory production, marketing, and more. Without a board of shareholders to report to, Sarah didn't lose time socializing ideas, garnering consensus, or answering board member objections. Instead, with concentrated executive power, she was able to move fast and, in doing so, become the world's youngest female self-made billionaire in 2012.

Are we then just gluttons for punishment in the social good sector, determined to make progress as complicated as possible? Or is there a more compelling reason why nonprofits are governed by boards?

The Difference between the Salvation Army and Spanx

The fundamental difference between nonprofit organizations and for-profit companies is that the former exist to serve society while the latter exist primarily to serve shareholder interests. There are no individual owners or shareholders of nonprofits. Even a founder or a major donor doesn't have ownership rights in a nonprofit organization. The closest thing a nonprofit organization has to an owner, in fact, is the community, or said another way, society-at-large. In exchange for the charitable good that a nonprofit purposes to do for the community, they receive a full range of meaningful tax benefits in return. In the United States, 501(c)(3) organizations don't pay income tax, sales tax, or property tax, and contributions to charitable organizations are tax deductible.

Given the meaningful investment society makes in the operation of a nonprofit organization through favorable tax treatment, we look to members of the community to serve as trustees of its purpose and to protect society's interest in the work. In short, we entrust oversight of nonprofits to a group of individuals—almost always volunteers—who stand ready, willing, and able to serve as trustees of the organization's mission. This group of individuals is most commonly called the board of directors. The board accepts the responsibility for governing, shepherding, and supporting the organization's work as it seeks to fulfill its charitable purpose.

Consider the complexity of this leadership structure. Each board member has just one vote. The chief executive often serves on the board *ex officio* (Latin for "by virtue of one's office"). Sometimes the chief executive is granted voting power by the organization's bylaws, but sometimes not. Board members elect board officers: commonly a board chair, vice chair, treasurer, and secretary. These officers are generally assigned specific responsibilities in the organization's bylaws but, despite these enhanced obligations, are granted a solitary vote. The board chair is usually granted the power to appoint committee chairs who, in turn, have significant influence overseeing the function within the purview of their committee. In membership organizations, the membership as a whole will often elect board members rather than leave it to the board to identify their own.

Sound complicated? This leadership arrangement has been described by Jim Collins in *Good to Great and the Social Sectors* as a "complex governance and diffuse power structure"[3] and for good reason.

Board members, acting in their role, serve as fiduciaries of the organization. That means once they're elected to a governing board, these directors—individually and collectively—are legally and ethically required to act in the best interests of the organization. They are duty bound to exercise a high degree of care as they serve. This is a position of real responsibility, steeped in trust. Board members must stay informed, making thoughtful decisions, keeping faithful to the organization's mission, and acting with undivided loyalty to the nonprofit rather than in the pursuit of their own personal gain.

Board Member: The Job Description

There are four key areas of responsibility for board members, and they will fulfill these responsibilities through what we often refer to as the *Three Ts*—time, talent, and treasure.

FOUR KEY AREAS OF BOARD RESPONSIBILITY

Nonprofit boards accept the responsibility to perform four core functions as they help lead an organization in the governance role:

- Strategic Responsibility
- Fiduciary Responsibility
- Resource Responsibility
- Capacity-Building Responsibility

---

3   Jim Collins, Good to Great and the Social Sectors (New York: Harper, 2005), 10.

These four obligations provide a clear framework for the important work that nonprofit boards undertake. They safeguard the organization's financial and operational health, strategic direction, and adherence to its mission and values, all crucial for its success and impact.

Strategic Responsibility

Boards are instrumental in charting the course for the nonprofit's future. They engage in shaping the organization's mission and vision, long-term goals, and the strategies needed to achieve them.

The board works closely with the chief executive, senior staff, and other stakeholder groups to establish the strategic framework for the organization. The board is ultimately responsible for developing the mission statement—its core purpose. The board will often go further and describe an organizational vision, as well—a "North Star" statement describing what the world would look like if the mission was one day accomplished. These two statements provide the framework for building a multiyear plan that articulates the strategic direction of the organization's future trajectory of growth.

After the strategy is formally agreed to, the board is then responsible for ensuring that it comes to life. The strategic plan should not be a beautifully worded blueprint for the future that is stored somewhere on a bookshelf, never to be thought of again. Instead, it should be a constant reference point as management and the board make decisions, balance competing demands for resources, track progress, monitor successes and shortfalls, and make course corrections as needed.

The board is engaged most intently at the beginning and end of the strategic planning process. At the beginning, the board should do a deep dive into the operating landscape and then agree on the mission, vision, and high-level priorities that will serve as the framework for a strategic plan. The chief executive and senior staff will then play a leading role in building out the fine details of the strategic plan. Thereafter, the board will come back together to offer feedback, perhaps make targeted changes, and ultimately approve a final plan. In my view, defining the future of the organization's work is one of the most important and fulfilling responsibilities in governance.

Fiduciary Responsibility

A second core board obligation is to safeguard the organization's overall well-being. This means keeping a close eye on the organization's finances, ensuring it complies with all regulations, effectively supporting and overseeing the work of the chief executive, and making sure resources are used effectively to fulfill the mission.

A formal definition of "fiduciary" describes being invested with power or responsibility that is then exercised for the benefit of another person or persons. With this responsibility comes the obligation to act in the best interests of the beneficiaries, and not in self-interest. Attorneys have a fiduciary responsibility to their clients. Financial advisors have a fiduciary responsibility to those whose money they manage. Real estate agents are fiduciaries for the home buyers or sellers they represent. In the same way, nonprofit board members are legally and ethically bound to act in the best interests of the organization and the beneficiaries it serves.

Resource Responsibility

Generating resources and serving as stewards of those resources are at the heart of the board's role. This means driving both financial support and human capital into the organization.

Financial resources come from the board in the form of giving and fundraising. You'll likely have a lot of questions about what this looks like, and we'll get into it shortly. Keep in mind that the board should be driving *human* resources into the organization, as well, in the form of board candidates, committee members, volunteers, and other supporters of the work. Great board members are always on the lookout for others who might want to join them in supporting the organization's mission.

A Causie Story: Gretchen Slusser and Adam Stanley

Gretchen Slusser owned an IT consulting and global project management business and was also a big believer in giving back. Among other things, her company gave 10 percent of its profits every year to a cause. One of her biggest clients was a multinational insurance company, supporting a team led by global chief technology officer, Adam Stanley.

Aware that Adam is known to be an actively involved philanthropist in his community, Gretchen dropped by his office one day and asked him if he had any suggestions on where she might make her contribution that year. Adam reached over and grabbed a brochure sitting on the side of his desk—it was for CGLA.

Gretchen wasn't immediately taken by CGLA's mission to provide free legal assistance, so she decided to get a firsthand experience before donating by serving as a volunteer. The organization's office was conveniently located near her home, she had extra time to invest, and she wasn't going to give an organization $10,000 until she knew she believed in it.

CGLA's volunteer coordinator initially assigned Gretchen to serve as the backup receptionist, answering phones and greeting clients when they arrived to meet with their attorney. As she began to experience the deeply challenging and imperiling circumstances that CGLA's clients were facing, she became more and more committed to the organization's work. Over time, Gretchen escalated her volunteer time by joining the gala committee. Before long, she was all-in with CGLA. She'd found a new community of like-minded professionals working on a vital cause. When the executive director role at CGLA became available, Adam encouraged Gretchen to apply for the job, and, after a thorough interview and vetting process, she was hired to lead the organization.

Gretchen moved from knowing nothing about CGLA to becoming a volunteer, major donor, fundraiser, and then its executive director in two years' time, simply because a board member, Adam Stanley, pointed her in the direction of his cause.

Capacity-Building Responsibility

Board members contribute their professional expertise and hard-earned wisdom to strengthen the organization's capacity to succeed in its mission. This includes leveraging their professional skill set, knowledge, and life experience to contribute to the growth and enhancement of the nonprofit. A board of directors consisting of members with a wide array of skill sets and life experiences is well positioned to build the capacity of the organization, helping it exponentially grow its mission impact.

In board service, a Causie brings the wholeness of who they are to advance the mission. One of the interesting aspects of board service is that members do a lot of role-switching, often even in the span of the same board meeting. At times they serve as a *strategist*. At other times, as a *governor* or overseer. Often they're acting in the *supporter* and ambassador role. And then, from time to time, they're more like a *consultant*, leveraging their personal and professional expertise.

Board members play various roles:

- *Strategist*—shaping and monitoring strategy
- *Governor*—providing fiduciary oversight
- *Supporter*—driving resources into the organization
- *Consultant*—using one's expertise to strengthen the organization

The Three Ts of Nonprofit Board Service

In the nonprofit sector, we speak of the "Three Ts" asked of board members, namely, the personal investment of one's time, talent, and treasure. Let's explore each one in turn.

TIME

The first question that busy professionals in the process of exploring nonprofit board service will typically ask is: *How much time will it take?* Here's the good news: Because nonprofit board members are volunteer leaders, board service is structured for busy professionals like you who are doing this work in addition to their many other personal and professional commitments.

To be specific in answer to the question, however, one should plan to dedicate four to six hours a month in order to serve their organization effectively from a seat on the board. Some months are a bit more, some months a bit less, but in general, this is a solid baseline as you consider whether you have sufficient time to make the commitment. How will that time commitment typically map out?

- *Four to six two-hour board meetings/year:* A typical nonprofit will convene four to six two-hour meetings per year. A start-up organization may have as many as twelve meetings annually as they get their footing, but that frequency is very unusual. Attending board meetings in person is important, or via videoconferencing, when necessary. The board meeting is where the critical business of governance is accomplished. Think of the refrain from the musical, *Hamilton*: You "wanna be in the room where it happens!"

- *Four to six one-hour committee meetings/year:* Board members are usually assigned to serve on at least one board committee. Committees meet between board meetings and are designed to delve more deeply into a specific area such as finance, strategy, programs, personnel, marketing, or fundraising.

- *Two to four marquee events/year:* The board should show up in force at the organization's big events each year. These include splashy experiences like the annual gala, the groundbreaking on the new wing of the building, the graduation ceremony for participants in the program, or the opening night performance. Board member attendance will demonstrate the board's high level of engagement, encourage the staff, and demonstrate to funders and the community that the board is deeply invested in the work.

- *Preparation for meetings:* Doing the "homework" of board service may not be the most exciting responsibility, but it's very important. Before each meeting, the organization's leadership will typically send the board a packet of materials (sometimes called the "board docket") that includes the meeting agenda, prior meeting minutes, financial reports, and lots of additional information on topics to be covered. Reviewing these materials in advance is mission critical to serving as an engaged, productive, thoughtful board member in the meeting.

- *Active engagement between meetings:* Candidates for board service often envision governance as attending a series of meetings. They visualize a host of reports, votes of "yay" or "nay," and a few moments of inspiration. That's certainly part of it, but this final aspect of how board members use their time is what sets great board members apart from good board members. Great board members engage *between* meetings. They've made board service a part of their personal and professional identity. They're thinking about and acting on the organization and its mission as they move through life.

Examples of How Great Board Members Can Engage between Meetings

- Invite a staff member from your nonprofit to a sporting event, concert, or another outing as a way of expressing appreciation for their hard work.

- Check in with the chief executive to see how they're doing, and ask if there's anything you can do to lighten their load.

- Participate in one of the organization's monthly volunteer events.

- Surprise the staff with a pizza lunch at the office.

- Attend an industry conference with the chief executive to become more familiar with the organization's programmatic subject matter.

- Host a lunch meeting with donors or foundation officers at your office to demonstrate board buy-in.

- Flag newsworthy items that might impact the work of the organization with a relevant staff member.

- Take a fellow board member to dinner to build a stronger relationship.

The professionals that my firm, Cause Strategy Partners, has placed on nonprofit boards through our signature program, BoardLead, report that just over one-third of their board service time involves attending meetings. The remainder of their governance work is invested in a healthy balance that includes engaging in fundraising activities, marketing the organization among their network, performing functions like financial oversight and strategy shaping at board retreats, and active participation in the volunteer program.

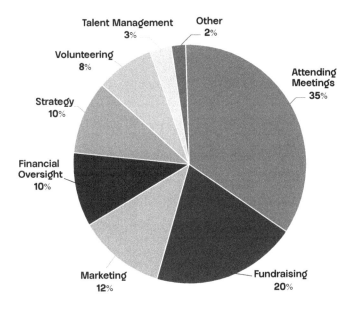

Simply put, notable board service often happens outside the four walls of the boardroom. It happens between board meetings. It occurs when a board member is serving as an ambassador of the organization. It happens when a director is on-site, getting firsthand experience with the core work of the organization. Great board service is self-generated, not driven by a board meeting agenda.

TALENT

Nonprofit board members have the opportunity to leverage the key professional skills they've cultivated over their career. The same functions that are necessary to run a for-profit company—human resources, legal, finance, marketing, and technology, for example—are also required to operate a nonprofit organization. The *way* a professional engages their expertise as a board member, however, is quite different from their day job.

An executive or team leader performs a number of roles in their work: setting performance goals, overseeing the day-to-day operation, making critical decisions, allocating resources, and managing a profit and loss (P&L) statement, to name a few. When that same professional steps into the boardroom, however, they need to shift their mindset from executing to governing. The skills that lead to success as an executive are quite different from the success drivers for a nonprofit board member who serves in a governance role.

I think of the board member role as a champion of functional area excellence, committing to strengthen the organization's operation in the professional skill set area that person knows best. Rather than *doing* the work of the organization, a board member should serve as a thought partner with the chief executive and any staff members with responsibilities in their core area of expertise.

When I serve on a nonprofit board, for example, I'm committed to ensuring that the governance function of the board is effective, reflects best practices, and is continually improving. Since nonprofit governance is my professional area of expertise, I can't abide serving on a board that has a governance function operating far below the standard of excellence I'm committed to in my work. I'm much less helpful in ensuring a well-run human resources or technology function at the organizations I serve as a board member. Those areas are outside of my core expertise. But I take great pride in helping the area I do know well—the governance function—thrive.

TREASURE

Giving and fundraising are almost always at the top of the list of things that board candidates want to know more about. In the simplest terms possible, there are three key considerations to keep in mind before raising your hand for a nonprofit board seat.

1. *You must give:* 100 percent of the board will be expected to make an annual personal financial contribution.

2. *Be prepared to fundraise:* Board members are usually expected to participate in the organization's fundraising effort.

3. *You may be asked to generate a specific amount:* Many organizations request that board members give and fundraise an agreed-upon minimum amount of money each year, called the give/get.

Let's take a closer look at each one of these three expectations.

Giving

Board members must make a personally meaningful financial contribution to the organization each year. Because nonprofit organizations are charitable in nature and raise money to cover the costs associated with running the organization, board members should set the pace each year by making a personally meaningful gift to support the work. Board members usually serve as fundraisers as well, and it would be unseemly to ask others to contribute to the cause if they themselves hadn't demonstrated a personal commitment to do so first. Moreover, when a nonprofit applies for a foundation grant, they'll often be asked to respond to the question, "What percentage of the board of directors made a personal financial contribution last fiscal year?" If the response is not 100 percent, it could serve as an impediment to being awarded a grant.

The next question, of course, is rather straightforward: How much? For starters, this isn't the contribution one makes to a friend's social media birthday campaign to support their favorite cause. Rather, this contribution should be personally meaningful and, in my view, sacrificial in nature. Board members should feel the gift in their gut when they make it each year. They might even earmark the contribution in their annual household budget, given its size. Why? Well, a board member's contribution is often larger than one's annual household utilities, holiday gift budget, or annual pet expenses.

Whatever the size of the contribution, here's a good test to use: *Will you be proud of the amount you gave when the chief executive or board chair calls you to express their gratitude? Will you think to yourself, "I should have done more?"* For many, that amount is $500–$1,000. For others, it's $5,000. For a select few, the gift might reach into the five, six, or even seven figures.

Whatever that number is for you, commit to making a stretch donation each year.

Fundraising

Board members must be prepared to participate in the organization's fundraising effort. Now I know that sentence sends shivers up the spines of many candidates exploring board service. The idea of making a personal donation doesn't cause most people anxiety and fear, but asking other people for money? That's an entirely different story. Putting one's hand out for a donation doesn't rank on anyone's top ten list of favorite things to do! Let's briefly demystify this responsibility now, but we will discuss it in much greater detail in chapter 8, setting you up to become a fundraising pro.

Every year, a nonprofit organization needs to generate the revenue required to compensate the staff with salary and benefits, pay the rent or mortgage, run the programs and services of the organization, and cover a host of other expenses. To do so, in addition to any public funding from government contracts and earned income (such as membership dues, ticket prices, or fee-based services), they must fundraise from private sources including individuals, corporations, and private foundations.

Most nonprofits have a robust infrastructure in place for this fundraising effort, and board members are simply asked to plug in. There's the annual gala, the silent auction, the 5K run, the end-of-year holiday campaign, the Giving Tuesday effort, the wine-tasting event, and more. Many organizations will have a dedicated fundraising (or development) team, including a staff member who works with board members, to help each one achieve their giving and fundraising goals for the year. The key is the willingness of board members—fueled by mission passion—to offer their best efforts in securing contributions from those in their network.

The Give/Get

Finally, board candidates should always be clear on exactly what's expected of them in the "treasure" category of responsibilities before standing for election to the board. Some organizations don't have a specific amount of money that they ask board members to give and fundraise each year, but many do. In fact, in my experience, a significant majority of nonprofit organizations now articulate a minimum amount that each board member is asked to commit to bringing in each year through the combination of their giving and fundraising— affectionately known as "the give/get." This approach allows for flexibility in how individual board members will achieve their financial goals for the year. One board member may lean into their personal contribution, and another may rely more heavily on their fundraising outcomes, but both commit to meet the minimum expectation established for all board members.

A Give/Get Example

Angela serves on the board of directors of Nonprofit, Inc. Each board member commits to a "give/get" of $5,000 per year. Angela has set up an automatic withdrawal of $100/month through the organization's online contributions system or $1,200/year. With that generous monthly contribution, Angela is well on her way toward achieving her board expectation. Angela's employer has a gift-matching policy that matches all employee contributions to nonprofit organizations, up to $1,000 per year. This brings her annual contribution to $2,200. Angela also sells ten $200 tickets to the annual gala totaling $2,000, and a close friend makes a generous $5,000 grant from her family foundation. Angela has generated $9,200 for Nonprofit, Inc., far surpassing her $5,000 give/get for the year.

Angela's fellow board member, Jared, has had a tough financial year. Jared lost his job seven months ago and is still searching for his next opportunity. Jared and his partner have also stepped in to help raise their nephew, while Jared's sister works through a personal challenge. Jared informs Nonprofit, Inc.'s development officer that he will make a stretch gift of $500 this year, despite these life circumstances, even though he has traditionally given $5,000 out of pocket in the past. He commits to work hard identifying silent auction items from his broad network and will host a gathering of friends in his home over the holidays with an "ask" to support the work. These efforts generate more than the remaining $4,500 and, in turn, satisfy his give/get.

The Benefits of Serving on a Nonprofit Board

As you can see, board members give a lot in service to their organization, but they also receive a great deal in return; board service isn't a one-way proposition. As you take steps forward as a Causie in your board service journey, keep in mind the many benefits of serving on a nonprofit board. Don't be afraid to grab ahold of them. While your passion for the mission is driving your decision to serve, you should also make use of the opportunities that flow back to you as you serve your cause from a board seat.

How can you benefit from serving on a board?

- Your wisdom and professional skills are needed and will be put to good use.

- You'll learn new skills in the boardroom across organizational functions.

- You'll build strong relationships with a network of exceptional, like-minded individuals who share your values and interests.

- You'll deepen your understanding of an issue area you care about.

- You'll effect change on your cause as you strengthen an organization doing work to advance that cause.

- You'll develop your leadership profile, adding positions to your professional bio, résumé, and LinkedIn profile.

- You'll just feel *good*, knowing you are making a difference in the world!

These are substantial returns on your personal investment of time, talent, and treasure. Board service offers personal and professional rewards that you should fully embrace. That's nothing to feel guilty about. Seize this opportunity to enhance yourself, your community, and your cause, all at the same time.

Putting Your Passion into Action

So, now you've got the basics of what board service is all about. The next chapter will describe our secret sauce at Cause Strategy Partners and BoardLead: what we call *The BoardLeader Way*. What are the qualities and behaviors that distinguish good board members from great ones? This is one of my favorite topics, and we will cover it next. See you in chapter 5.

Reflection Questions

- Which one of the four board member roles feels like the best fit for you? Which one will be a personal growth curve?

    - Strategist

    - Governor

    - Supporter

    - Consultant

- Are you prepared to engage in the Three Ts of nonprofit board service?

    - *Time:* Can you dedicate four to six hours/month to serving an organization?

    - *Talent:* What professional skill set or life experiences will you leverage as a board member? In what area can you be a champion of functional area excellence?

    - *Treasure:* Are you prepared to make a personally meaningful annual contribution each year and participate in the fundraising effort? What give/get amount would you be prepared to commit to if elected to a nonprofit board?

- What would it look like for you to deliver unique value to a nonprofit between meetings, outside of the boardroom?

Chapter Five

A Higher Standard of Board Service

In order to be irreplaceable, one must always be different.

—COCO CHANEL

Soon after I left my job to launch Cause Strategy Partners, I was at lunch with a friend who is himself a former nonprofit founder and CEO. After describing the board matching, training, and support program I was beginning to build, his immediate response was: "Rob, do the sector a favor. If you're going to put your time and energy into this, do something different. Be disruptive. Nonprofits don't need any more mediocre board members."

His guidance was direct, to be sure, and I also knew exactly where he was coming from. Having spent my career working for and serving on the boards of a number of nonprofit organizations, I've seen my share of ineffective, disengaged, phone-it-in board members. Unfortunately, the data support this reality. The *2021 Leading with Intent: BoardSource Index of Nonprofit Board Practices*[4] asked nonprofit chief executives and board chairs to rate their board's performance across a range of areas on a four-point scale. The average score nonprofit leaders gave their board for level of commitment and involvement was

---

4   BoardSource, "Leading with intent: BoardSource index of nonprofit board practices," 2021, 16, https://delawarenonprofit.org/wp-content/uploads/2022/09/2021-Leading-with-Intent-Report.pdf.

a disappointing 2.60. On a letter-grading scale, that equates to a C–, settling right into the center of the Land of Mediocrity.

My friend's plea was directly aligned with one of my core reasons for beginning this work. I had absolutely no interest in helping professionals land a board seat for the purpose of getting their headshot on an organization's website or their name on the letterhead. Rather, I wanted to help nonprofits thrive in pursuit of their mission by developing board members who would bring the very best of themselves to board leadership. But how could I ensure that the professionals we worked with would meet high standards of governance practices? With lackluster performance as the norm, what could I do to ensure that the candidates placed through my new enterprise would serve with excellence, aiming to meet an elevated form of board service? In looking for a solution, two experiences from my past came to mind.

"If That's Not You, Please Stand Up and Leave Right Now."

In my first job out of law school, I served as the director of legal education for an organization based in Harlem called Legal Outreach, Inc. Once a year, we would recruit law students from nearby Columbia Law School to mentor and coach the high school students enrolled in Legal Outreach's five-year college-bound program. These volunteer law students would assist our kids in preparing for constitutional debates and mock trials, helping them understand the relevant law, apply a fact pattern, craft compelling arguments, and fine-tune their delivery. We trained our volunteer law students to never give our students the answers but rather to work alongside them as they processed the materials and, with coaching, help them figure solutions out for themselves. In other words, we didn't want "saviors" who would drop in with all of the answers. We wanted patient coaches who believed in the potential of our students and who would put in the time and effort to cultivate their growth.

The program began each year with volunteer recruitment. With a classroom full of bright law students assembled to learn more about the opportunity, Legal Outreach's cofounder and executive director, James B. O'Neal, would explain what the commitment involved, the methodology they would be expected to use in coaching students, and more. Then, he would wrap up with a direct charge that went something like this: "Our college-bound students deserve excellence. They deserve to be believed in and challenged in the same way you were when you were in high school. If you can't follow through on the commitments I've just outlined, please stand up and leave right now."

The first time I heard James invite people to exit the room who couldn't live up to his high standards for our students, I cringed a bit. It seemed somewhat unceremonious to me to be so blunt when a roomful of terribly busy Columbia Law students took time at the end of a busy day to learn about what was, after all, a volunteer opportunity. But after I saw the dozens of law students we selected coach our students so passionately, consistently, and effectively over weeks and weeks, I understood his approach. Setting the very highest of expectations at the outset led to truly exceptional performance, even for a group of wildly busy, overwhelmed law students.

The HP Way

Many years ago, I read Carly Fiorina's book *Tough Choices*,[5] a memoir that documented her time as the CEO of Hewlett-Packard (HP). I learned that the founders of the company—Bill Hewlett and

---

5   Carly Fiorina, Tough Choices: A Memoir (New York: Portfolio, 2007).

Dave Packard—along with other company leaders, articulated the company's culture, management philosophy, and values in a statement they called *The HP Way*. This statement served as a guiding force for the company as it grew in size and reputation, articulating its commitment to approaches like "management by walking around," employee empowerment, long-term perspective, and a focus on quality. *The HP Way* not only proved to be a powerful foundational force for the company but had broader influence outside the firm, as well, shaping how the business world thinks about management philosophy.

The BoardLeader Way

As I grappled with the challenge of ensuring that the professionals we would work with through BoardLead would wholeheartedly embrace the highest standards of governance, I landed on a four-part solution, influenced by both James B. O'Neal and the founders of Hewlett-Packard. First, I would clearly articulate what full board engagement looks like and give it a name: *The BoardLeader Way*. Second, before working with a board candidate, we would require them to sign on the dotted line, formally committing up front to perform board service consistent with the elevated expectations outlined in *The BoardLeader Way*. Third, we would provide robust governance training for the professionals we work with to ensure that they have the knowledge, tools, and insights necessary to be effective in board governance from day one. Finally, we would build in accountability by evaluating the performance of every professional elected to a board through our work, after both one and two years of service.

As a founder, one gets some things wrong and some things right. This one I got right! The combination of articulating high expectations, requiring a formal commitment, providing access to effective training at the outset, and building in accountability has proven to be a key aspect of BoardLead's secret sauce. Nearly every day we hear from a chief executive or board chair of one of our nonprofit partners, thanking us for connecting them to a professional who is driving significant impact from their seat on the board. We have an internal Slack channel called *#boardlove* where our team members regularly post these notes of gratitude and praise. I also have an email file where I stash away the many expressions of appreciation from our partners. These successes, in many ways, track all the way back to the beginning—this early decision to create *The BoardLeader Way* and institutionalize the four-pronged approach setting clear expectations for full board engagement.

The BoardLeader Way

- Engage robustly in board meetings
- Serve on at least one board committee
- Maintain a near-perfect meeting attendance record
- Contribute a personally meaningful and sacrificial annual gift
- Participate actively in all fundraising efforts
- Leverage your skills and network to drive impact
- Use your power to advance diversity, equity, and inclusion
- Complete each elected term

Every board member should stretch themselves, committing to a high standard of full engagement. By meeting this standard of excellence, board members demonstrate that they have the dedication required to rise to board leadership positions and increase their impact.

As you embark on your board service journey, I sincerely hope that you, too, will aim for a very high standard of engagement—not the floor but the ceiling. The floor is mediocrity: attending an occasional meeting, passively participating, rarely thinking about the work between meetings, requiring the staff to track you down to make an annual contribution, or making little effort to fundraise and generate financial support. That's a C– performance. You wouldn't aim for average in your day job, nor should you give a half-baked effort to the important role of board leadership.

Full board engagement is my personal passion, the reason my company exists, and the reason I'm writing this book. It's my sincere hope that every professional who reads this will serve in a manner that reflects *The BoardLeader Way*, seek out governance training to be ready to serve effectively, and hold themselves accountable to consistently strong board leadership performance.

What Nonprofits Need

A 2015 study conducted by BoardSource found that less than one out of every five nonprofit chief executives "strongly agree that they have the right board members to effectively oversee and govern their organizations."[6] To make matters worse, building a talented board is a real challenge in the nonprofit sector: one-third of chief executives and more than half of nonprofit board chairs indicate that it's difficult to find new board members.[7] There are two leading reasons cited for this challenge: difficulty finding individuals with the desired skill set and a limited supply of individuals interested in serving.[8]

---

6   BoardSource, "Leading with intent," 13.

7   Ibid., 30.

8   Ibid., 31.

These findings don't surprise me. Having served for more than a decade as an executive director of two nonprofit organizations, I'm keenly aware of the overwhelming demands on the time and attention of nonprofit chief executives. They might spend a third of their time fundraising and another third overseeing programs and staff. The last third is composed of a huge range of activities, including partnering with the board, shaping strategy, cultivating strategic partnerships, handling media requests, overseeing finances, and dealing with a dozen unexpected (and often unwelcome) surprises each day.

With such a full slate of responsibilities, it's challenging for nonprofit chief executives to find the time to go into the world and identify strong potential candidates for the board. To be clear, it's ultimately the responsibility of the board of directors to elect their fellow board members. This role must not be delegated to the CEO. Even so, given the limited amount of time board members have to invest in board development on top of the full range of governance responsibilities, many boards rely heavily on the chief executive to surface names for consideration.

Perhaps even more common, a board committee will take charge of the candidate identification process but limit their search to the existing network of current board members. This tends to lead to nonprofit board development processes that are limited in scope, clubby, and nonstrategic. Rather than cast a wide net likely to identify top candidates from a broad array of backgrounds, communities, industries, identities, and experiences, I've too often seen the governance or nominating committee chair ask at a board meeting, "Does anybody know anybody who might consider joining our board?"

That, friend, is exactly how board development should *not* be done. This short-cut approach serves to perpetuate a board composition that's homogenous rather than powerful in its diversity and reflective of the community served.

From the board candidate's vantage point, the most common approach for finding a nonprofit board can be captured in three words: *sit and wait*. Despite having an interest in serving on a board, most people don't take steps forward either because (a) they don't know what's involved, (b) they don't know where to start, or (c) they don't believe they have the requisite background to qualify for a board position. Instead, talented professionals simply wait until a friend taps them on the shoulder and says, "Hey, I'm on the board of this charity. Wanna join me?"

We need to shake up this ineffective approach to board development, for nonprofits and candidates alike. In this traditional approach, a governance committee solicits candidate names from current board members, decides on whom to approach, and then begins the process of reaching out to assess the interests of those on the shortlist. These candidates may or may not have a particular interest in the cause or the organization. Oftentimes, the first time the candidate has even heard about the nonprofit or has been invited to get involved is when they're asked to consider joining the board. This means they skip over the many stages of escalating involvement discussed in chapter 3, such as serving as a donor, volunteer, fundraiser, or advisor. Essentially, the traditional strategy relies on approaching and then wooing an untested candidate to try to get them elected to the board—often on a tight time frame—without any real proof point of demonstrable interest in the mission or cause. When you stop and think about it, that's a rather risky proposition, don't you think?

My goal is to reverse this process entirely. My firm's BoardLead program starts by asking professionals to select their top-choice nonprofit rather than having our participating nonprofits select the candidate. We then offer our candidates training, make the introduction, and set them loose to make the case for how they'll serve and advance the mission of the organization. In other words, the candidate chooses and then woos the nonprofit.

That simple shift in the power dynamics of the board development process has turned BoardLead into a trusted partner. Nonprofit organizations come back to us, year after year, to meet more candidates interested in their cause. Incredibly, more than 40 percent of our BoardLeaders are elected or appointed to a leadership role on their board within the first year of service.

This innovative model has really worked. We have won numerous awards from mayors, social impact industry groups, trade magazines, and nonprofit organizations. In 2022, I was humbled and honored to be named a Top 100 Impact CEO by Big Path Capital, an investment bank focused on advancing a sustainable economy. The MO 100 Top Impact CEO Ranking "celebrates leaders who are leveraging the engine of capitalism to create shared prosperity."[9] Its rankings are based on a company's pace of growth, profitability, and overall impact. By proactively connecting candidates to a nonprofit at the center of their passion and by asking them to commit to a high standard of board performance, we see exceptional outcomes for both nonprofits and the professionals we work with.

Rather than wait for that moment when one of your friends asks if you might consider joining the board of an organization that they serve, what if you took control of the process instead? I want you—*when you're ready*—to be intentional about how you will invest your time in service. I don't want you to rely on happenstance like so many do. I don't want you to commit to an organization that doesn't sit at the center of your value system. Rather, I want you to be proactive and

---

9   "Momentum 100," MO, accessed April 5, 2024, https://mo-summit.com/mo100-ranking/.

make magic happen. Heed Winnie the Pooh's sage advice to Piglet: "You can't stay in your corner of the forest waiting for others to come to you. You have to go to them sometimes."[10] This is a completely different approach from the one used by the vast majority of people hoping to one day serve on a board. So, the first thing that needs to happen is a mindset shift: stop waiting.

The Final Checklist

You've identified your cause. You've found a target organization to serve as your Causie home. You know the various ways to support a nonprofit organization and have positioned yourself for a potential board seat. You know the basics of what nonprofit board service is all about, and you're committed to serving in a way that reflects the highest standards of governance, captured in *The BoardLeader Way*. Now, before you take the governance leap, there are three important questions to answer. This is your final gut check. If you can wholeheartedly answer each question in the affirmative, you're ready for board service.

- Am I passionate about this organization's mission?

- Will I show up as a board member who is consumed with mission achievement?

- Do I have a vision for how I can use my personal strengths to make an impact?

Let's look at each one.

AM I PASSIONATE ABOUT THIS ORGANIZATION'S MISSION?

When nonprofit leaders are asked to choose from a list of characteristics that board candidates might bring to their organization, the

---

10   A.A. Milne, Winnie-the-Pooh (New York: Dutton Books for Young Readers, 1988).

primary priority is crystal clear: *passion for the mission.* As you can see in this graph, despite the very compelling list of criteria that candidates can bring to board service—a desirable professional skill, a prominent reputation in the community, the ability to fundraise, a broad network, or a demographic background that will contribute to diversity on the board, for example—at the top of the list is passion for the mission.[11]

Priorities in Board Recruitment

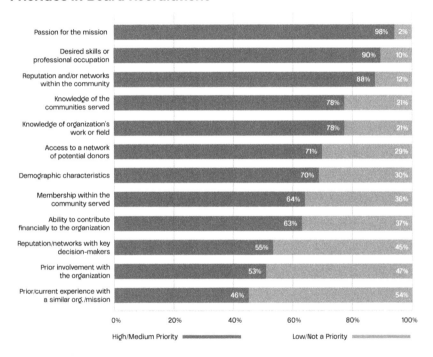

	High/Medium Priority	Low/Not a Priority
Passion for the mission	98%	2%
Desired skills or professional occupation	90%	10%
Reputation and/or networks within the community	88%	12%
Knowledge of the communities served	78%	21%
Knowledge of organization's work or field	78%	21%
Access to a network of potential donors	71%	29%
Demographic characteristics	70%	30%
Membership within the community served	64%	36%
Ability to contribute financially to the organization	63%	37%
Reputation/networks with key decision-makers	55%	45%
Prior involvement with the organization	53%	47%
Prior/current experience with a similar org./mission	46%	54%

We hear the same thing when our team interviews the leaders of nonprofits seeking board candidates through BoardLead. When we ask board chairs and chief executives what we should prioritize in identifying candidates for their board, the first response is almost always the same: "Please only send us candidates who are passionate about our mission."

---

11   BoardSource, "Leading with intent," 30.

This comes as no surprise. Nonprofit organizations are mission driven. They are for-purpose entities. The mission statement is the central, guiding force for everything the organization will do. Before standing for election to a nonprofit board, be certain that the mission of the organization resonates deeply with you.

WILL I SHOW UP AS A BOARD MEMBER WHO IS CONSUMED WITH MISSION ACHIEVEMENT?

Passion for the mission is necessary but not sufficient. I've spent a lot of time in nonprofit boardrooms over the years. Based on my experience, too few organizations could ever be accused of having board members who are consumed with mission achievement. It can be somewhat disheartening. There are many ways to spot a disengaged board.

- *Board members show up late or not at all.* The board chair or CEO is reduced to calling and texting board members as the meeting is set to start, begging them to dial in so that they can reach quorum.

- *Board members show up but don't engage.* The meeting becomes a show-and-tell affair featuring the chief executive. Board members don't ask questions, dig for deeper understanding, challenge assumptions, or offer ideas.

- *Board members are not prepared.* They don't have the meeting packet of materials in front of them or, if they do, haven't read them. As a consequence, they don't have the information they need to have a meaningful understanding of the issues, and they don't have the data they need to make good decisions.

- *There's a "trust-and-hope" mentality regarding financial oversight.* When the treasurer provides a summary of the quarterly financials, few board members follow along. Many don't even feign interest by at least opening the reports. Rather than attempting to understand the financial position of the organization, they outsource the responsibility to others.

Frankly, I will never understand how someone can take on a fiduciary role on a nonprofit board—accepting the responsibility to govern, shepherd, and support a social good organization doing vital work in the community—and then become a no-show, or disengaged, or uninvolved, or drain-on-the-resources type of board member.

Let's paint another picture. What does a board member consumed with mission impact look like? To explore this together, let's work through an exercise.

South Bronx United

I'm a big fan of an organization called South Bronx United, founded by Andrew So in 2009, which provides support, education, and athletic opportunities to young people in the South Bronx. The birthplace of hip-hop and home to the New York Yankees, the South Bronx is a diverse and vibrant borough that gave the world a wealth of famous leaders, artists, athletes, and musicians, including General Colin Powell, Al Pacino, Jennifer Lopez, and my favorite major leaguer of all time, Reggie Jackson.

South Bronx United offers a range of youth development programs, including soccer leagues, afterschool academic support, assistance with the college application process, mentoring, and leadership development. The first sentence of their mission statement describes what they aim to accomplish.

> *South Bronx United uses soccer as a tool for social change aiming to help youth build character, teamwork, and leadership so that they can succeed in high school, college, careers, their community, and beyond.*

Now let's transport ourselves to the South Bronx. Imagine you're a board member of this organization. You're sitting at a conference room table in the organization's office on River Avenue alongside twenty fellow board members.

Let's also assume that you're a board member who is *consumed* with mission impact. You're not a wallflower, no-show, drain-the-resources kind of board member. Instead, you deeply believe in the South Bronx United mission and want to do everything in your power to bring it to life—to change the lives of the kids in the program.

As a board member consumed with mission impact, what are three questions you might want to explore in a board meeting? Referencing the mission statement earlier, what do you want to know? Jot your three questions in the following space.

1.

2.

3.

I've led this exercise in rooms full of board candidates, and I've heard a range of responses. "How many students are enrolled in the program this year?" is a common one, but it's not the question a board member consumed with mission impact would focus on. In fact, the answer to that question won't speak to how students are being impacted by the program at all. It offers information on headcount (sometimes affectionately referred to as the "butts-in-the-seat" number), but it says nothing about how the kids' lives are being changed and how the mission is being accomplished.

South Bronx United's mission statement describes the impact the organization seeks. It talks about building character, teamwork, and leadership so that the kids can succeed in high school, college, careers, and in their community. Impact questions will connect to those purposes. For example:

- What percentage of our seniors graduated from high school last year, and how does that compare to the benchmark high school graduation rate in the South Bronx? Did the graduation rate for our students go up or down this year compared with the last year? What can we do to strengthen this outcome?

- What is our definition of "character," and how does it shape our programming? How do we measure this objective? Do we have a benchmark? How will we know if we are succeeding or failing in this important purpose?

- What does it look like for our kids to experience success in college? What data do we use and how do we track it? What can we add to our programs and services that will strengthen their college readiness even more, further increasing their chances of success?

These are the questions of a board member consumed with mission impact. When you land on a board, I hope you'll demonstrate a deep level of commitment to mission impact, discontent with the status quo, curiosity about how things work, and an expectation to receive the data, reports, and information necessary to track success.

DO I HAVE A VISION FOR HOW I CAN USE MY PERSONAL STRENGTHS TO MAKE AN IMPACT?

I once met with a senior vice president at a Fortune 20 company who led a team of two hundred employees. She had a big job, overseeing functions that included product, marketing, operations, and finance. Her team brought in more than $1 billion in annual recurring revenue. Needless to say, I was wildly impressed with her background and couldn't wait to get her plugged into a board at the center of her passion. When we began the conversation, however, I was surprised by her lack of confidence as to whether she was a good fit to serve. She explained that she was interested in addressing the homelessness crisis in her city but felt like she had little to offer as a sales executive. "Rob, I don't know anything about homelessness. I honestly don't know how I can be of help as a board member." I succeeded, for the most part, in not chuckling in reply. I not only respected her humility but also thought to myself, "She's a dream candidate for a board and just doesn't see it yet."

Lacking subject matter expertise in a nonprofit's program area is not—I repeat, is *not*—an impediment to serving effectively from a seat on the board. In fact, nonprofits are usually stocked full with subject matter experts: the chief executive and the entire program staff, for starters. While it's certainly helpful to have some experts on the board who know the issue area the organization is working on very deeply, it's not a prerequisite for board service. *Why?* Because nonprofits also look to their board to provide professional expertise in the functions required to run an organization: finance, legal, HR, marketing, technology, and the like. The attributes you need most are a commitment to the work and an eagerness to learn. As you serve on a board, you will develop subject matter expertise as well.

Now, the manner in which you leverage your wisdom and skills will be different from how you apply them in your day job. At work, you execute. If you serve in an executive role, you're focused on leading a team and overseeing the work. If you're earlier in your career, you're likely charged with doing the work. But in the nonprofit boardroom, you're doing neither. Board work is a legislative-like function.

One thing I enjoy about board service is having the opportunity to observe successful leaders collaborate effectively with one another. Despite their individual reputations, gravitas, and leadership prowess, when they step into a boardroom, they serve shoulder to shoulder with one another, as peers. In the boardroom, they're governors, not executives. To be effective, they have to employ a different leadership style than the one that makes them successful in their career. They must unlock new ways to drive value from their seat on the board.

Can a leader, then, have influence on a board when they are just one of many? Yes, absolutely. As Frances Hesselbein, former CEO of the Girl Scouts of the United States, points out in *Good to Great and the Social Sectors*, you just have to know where to find it.[12] Hesselbein identifies a number of ways to have influence operating in an environment without concentrated executive power:

- *The power of inclusion:* Influential board members value the perspectives of others.

- *The power of shared interests:* Influential board members are not looking out for their self-interest but rather are consumed with the organization's shared interests.

- *The power of language:* Influential board members are persuasive communicators.

---

12   Jim Collins, *Good to Great and the Social Sectors: Why Business Thinking Is Not the Answer* (New York: Harper, 2005).

- *The power of coalition:* Influential board members play well with others who, in turn, are eager to work together in common cause.

I would add to this list four additional drivers of board influence:

- *The power of full engagement:* Influential board members set the pace for others as they contribute their time, talent, and treasure to the organization.

- *The power of connection:* Influential board members invest in building meaningful relationships with peers rooted in respect, authenticity, trust, and candor.

- *The power of initiative:* Influential board members step up when there's a need they can help solve.

- *The power of insight:* Influential board members listen to others carefully and, when they do speak, share original ideas that advance the conversation.

As you begin your board service journey, I encourage you to develop a personal vision for how you'll drive significant impact from your seat on the board. You already have what it takes to be a governance game changer. Lean into your strengths while starting with a learning mindset. As you learn the subject matter of the organization's work and leverage these drivers of influence, you'll become immensely important to the organization and its ability to make an impact.

Throwing Your Hat in the Ring

Alright, you're ready to go. It's time to put yourself forward for a board seat at your target organization that will serve as your cause area home. The next step is yours. It's time to make your interest in deepening your involvement known.

I ended up on the board of Nonprofit New York by asking a then-serving board member, Sandy Lamb, out to lunch. I'd attended a number of the organization's convenings, and the nonprofit I was serving as executive director benefited from their programs and services. This exposure strengthened my belief in the importance of Nonprofit New York's work in my city. I felt ready to engage more deeply. Over a Caesar salad and a Diet Coke, I asked Sandy what board service involved and wondered out loud if my personal and professional background might be a good fit.

With her encouragement and after making an introduction, I had a follow-up lunch meeting with the executive director, who engaged me in a similar conversation. After a few more steps in the organization's vetting process, I was elected to the board of directors and am now in my twelfth year of service. Nonprofit New York has served as home to one of my primary causes, developing the capacity of nonprofit organizations in my city. This journey began when I raised my hand, inquiring whether I might be a good fit for the organization's board.

From your vantage point as a board candidate, the process begins with a first meeting with the organization's leadership. It's important to remember, however, that a well-run nonprofit has a process in place for building the board. My firm, Cause Strategy Partners, has outlined a best-in-class board development process in a resource we call "Process Matters," which you can find in the Appendix. In this resource, we identify four stages in a well-designed board development process, each of which has two specific steps.

Preparation

- *Step One: Identify Needs:* Assess current board composition and prioritize gap areas.

- *Step Two: Identify Candidates:* Develop a diverse pool of talented candidates.

Exploration

- *Step Three: First Meeting:* Get to know candidates, provide key information, and assess alignment.

- *Step Four: Onsite Visit:* Give your candidates a memorable experience.

Vetting

- *Step Five: Additional Touch Points:* Win board buy-in and answer candidate questions.

- *Step Six: Agree on Nomination:* Make an informed decision and communicate clearly.

Engagement

- *Step Seven: Election:* Set high expectations for newly elected board members, asking them to stretch themselves.

- *Step Eight: Onboarding:* Give new board members training and resources to start strong.

In the next chapter, we dive deeply into the third and fourth steps of a well-run board development process: the first meeting and the on-site visit.

What's Next?

The final checklist is complete, all signs are affirmative, and you're ready to go! Now it's time to enter your target organization's board development process. In the next chapter, we'll focus on how to put your best foot forward as a board candidate, giving you the insights you need to soar through the introduction, vetting, nomination, and election process with flying colors. Let's set you up for success as you meet with the leadership of your target organization for the first time, exploring whether service on their board of directors might be a good fit for you.

Reflection Questions

- Are you prepared to stretch yourself, committing to the high standard of engagement outlined in *The BoardLeader Way?*

- As it relates to your target organization, can you say "yes" to all three items on the final checklist?

  ❏ I am deeply passionate about the mission.

  ❏ I'm prepared to serve as one consumed with mission achievement.

  ❏ I have a vision for how I will use my personal strengths to make an impact.

- Compared with your day job, what do you anticipate it will look like for you to unlock new ways to drive value from a seat on a nonprofit board?

Which drivers of board influence will come naturally to you? Which do you expect to represent a growth edge as you begin serving?

	Natural	Growth Edge
The power of inclusion	❏	❏
The power of shared interest	❏	❏
The power of language	❏	❏
The power of coalition	❏	❏
The power of full engagement	❏	❏
The power of connection	❏	❏
The power of initiative	❏	❏
The power of insight	❏	❏

Chapter
Six

Making a Great First Impression in the Vetting Process

Friendship is born at that moment when one person says to another, "What! You too? I thought I was the only one."

—C. S. LEWIS, *THE FOUR LOVES*

I'd known about Ted Chung for some time. As a prominent attorney in Chicago who was appointed general counsel to Illinois governor Pat Quinn, Ted had developed a reputation as a brilliant, dedicated, effective attorney and executive. Ted and I met in my office one morning in 2009 to explore whether my organization might be a good fit for Ted to serve as a board member.

That one-hour conversation was the most impressive first meeting I've ever had with a candidate exploring potential board service. What made it stand out from the rest? Ted showed up with incredibly high energy and demonstrable enthusiasm. His curiosity was unparalleled as he fired thoughtful question after thoughtful question at me to better understand the organization and its work. His careful due diligence showed through as he explored whether any responsibilities of board service would conflict with his role in state government. He communicated with conviction about the core work of our organization and how it aligned with his personal values around justice and mercy. After Ted left my office that day, I immediately called my board chair, telling him, "I've got a candidate you *have* to meet."

For many professionals, this first meeting in the get-to-know-one-another process can cause a high degree of anxiety. *Whom will I be meeting with? What are they going to ask me? What questions should I ask them? How can I put my best foot forward, demonstrating my fit for board leadership at the organization?* Ted's example during that introductory meeting became the cornerstone of a training resource we developed at Cause Strategy Partners. This resource has since been shared with thousands of board candidates we've connected with organizations over the years.

Perhaps this will be the first time you've interviewed for any position at a social impact organization, much less a board role. This chapter will help you prepare for a nonprofit's board candidate vetting process. Consider this your guidebook for what you should do from the moment you and your target nonprofit's leadership agree to discuss a board seat, into the first meeting, on to the site visit, and culminating with the decision on whether to stand for nomination to the board.

Planning for the First Meeting

As soon as you find out the name of the person you're meeting with, go to the organization's website and that individual's LinkedIn profile—essentially, cyberstalk them. Learn everything you can about the organization: its board, its staff, its programs, and its impact on the community it serves. How do they describe their set of programs and services? What bragging points do they put forward about their outcomes?

How many individuals are on the board? Its size will impact the way you serve. Generally speaking, in the nonprofit sector, a typical board has between fourteen and eighteen directors. A board considered small would have ten or fewer board members. Smaller boards tend to be more hands-on, amplifying the importance of your presence and personal involvement. A large board could have thirty or more members.

On a large board, you're likely to find more opportunities to drive impact at the committee level because there are so many voices around the table in full board meetings. Meanwhile, small boards likely do not have a committee structure in place. The smaller the board, the more likely it is to be a "working" board that guides and leads the organization but also goes beyond making decisions. Directors on a small board are more likely to be asked to roll up their sleeves and actively help with operational work from time to time. They don't just say what to do; they also get things done.

In addition, consider who is on the board. Look at their titles and employer affiliations. How will your background be additive to the overall industry and skill set mix currently represented in the boardroom?

In scheduling the first meeting, I strongly advise you to hold it in person. This conversation is about much more than gathering information. You're testing for culture fit, and so are they. You want to establish rapport with the leader you meet and begin to build an authentic, trusting relationship. Will you be able to work effectively and energetically with this board member, board chair, or chief executive? An in-person conversation provides a level of connectedness and depth that a virtual meeting simply cannot match.

Prepare Your Questions

One of the best ways to demonstrate your interest in the work is by leading with a high degree of curiosity. Show them you've done your homework. Make it obvious that you've engaged in research. Your questions should build on your foundation of due diligence. It will be off-putting if you ask questions that are obviously answerable on the organization's website. This may sound obvious, but I can't tell you how often I've seen this happen. Your questions should go beyond information that the organization already shares publicly with the world. If you demonstrate that you didn't prepare for this meeting, you're sending a signal that you won't come prepared to board or committee meetings either.

As you prepare, here's a hit list of questions you might ask in this first meeting. Choose those that are most relevant as you weigh whether this organization is indeed the right one for you.

PURPOSE AND STRATEGY

Questions that focus on purpose and strategy communicate your interest in the core mission. They also demonstrate that you understand you'll operate at the 10,000 feet level as a member of the board, not as a micromanaging leader.

- I've spent time on your website, of course, but can you tell me more about the organization's purpose? What's of top importance that isn't captured in the words of the mission statement?

- What does success look like? How is a client's life impacted through the programs and services?

- Is there a strategic plan in place? If so, what are the plan's primary objectives?

- What is your long-term vision for the future of this organization?

- What do you see as the greatest challenge the organization is facing right now?

STAFF AND FINANCES

Questions focused on the organization's finances telegraph you understand that financial oversight is an important fiduciary responsibility of the board. Compensation and benefits are typically the most significant expenses on a nonprofit's budget, so asking questions about the staff gives you important context about the overall operation.

- Is the organization's financial situation healthy? Are you likely to finish with a surplus or deficit this year?

- Is the organization on track to meet this year's revenue budget? What factors are influencing this?

- Is there sufficient diversity among the funding sources?

- Compared to the prior fiscal year, is revenue growing, declining, or staying flat?

- Have there been any challenges on the expense side of the budget in recent years? What caused them?

- How much cash does the organization have on hand?

- Have there been cash flow challenges in the recent past? What caused them?

- If you could only make one or two new hires next year, what roles would you add to the team?

- How is team morale? How would you describe the organization's culture?

BOARD SERVICE AND BOARD MEETINGS

Questions that explore the structure and makeup of the board demonstrate that, if elected, you would be an engaged director who is interested in making an impact. It is important to ask direct questions about what's expected of board members. Make sure you understand the full set of expectations early in the process so that there are no surprises later. You don't want to waste your time or theirs.

- How well is the board of directors functioning in your view?

- When, where, and how often are board meetings held?

- Is there a give or give/get requirement for board members? What percentage of the board meets those expectations?

- What is the range and average of board member giving each year? What about their fundraising outcomes?

- Given my background, what are your thoughts on which committee I might be the best fit for?

- What's the length of the term I'd be committing to? Are there term limits?

- As (CEO/board chair/a board member), how do you perceive your role as it relates to the board?

- How is the board championing diversity, equity, and inclusion within the organization and on the board itself?

- How are the perspectives of program beneficiaries and the community brought into boardroom conversations?

PERSONAL FIT AND READINESS

Questions that focus on your personal fit and readiness to serve on the board help the nonprofit's decision-makers begin to picture you in the role. They also demonstrate that you're eager to take the next step in the organization's board development process.

- Given your role, what do you *personally* need from board members?

- Are there any skill, life experience, or demographic gaps on the board that I might help fill?

- Do you have any concerns about my candidacy at this point? I'd love the chance to address them. I'm an open book, and I'm always eager to receive candid feedback.

Make a Great First Impression

Present yourself in the best possible light. Put your best foot forward, from punctuality and appropriate attire to thoughtful questions and insightful responses. Here's an expert tip: As early in the conversation as possible, get to know the individual you're meeting with on a deeper level. Put the focus on them. How did they first get involved in the organization? What motivates them to serve? How do they keep their passion for the mission burning bright?

Similarly, make sure you get the chance to explain *your* personal why behind your interest in the work. Go back to your written responses in chapters 2 and 3. Weave them together and share the brief backstory that speaks to your values and motivation. You'll likely discover deep commonalities with one another.

Share Your Personal Impact Hypothesis

At some point in the first meeting, try to share what I call your "personal impact hypothesis." This is your carefully considered proposition describing the potential influence or effect you believe you can have on the organization from a seat on the board. Describe how you believe you can uniquely drive value to the organization. You don't know everything you need to at this point, but at least try to have this hypothesis in mind for the conversation.

Consider, for example, how a board candidate sharing thoughts like these might resonate with a nonprofit leader who's eager to strengthen the organization's work.

- "I have an extensive network of colleagues and friends and I love throwing parties. I think I can be an effective fundraiser and friendraiser for the organization."

- "I've been an HR generalist for my entire career and feel like I've seen almost every situation in people operations. I might be a helpful thought partner with you and the team as sticky situations arise with employees."

- "I was born and raised in the community the organization serves. This is my home. It doesn't appear that our residents have much representation in the boardroom. I think I can be a helpful bridge between the community and this work."

- "I've helped companies scale substantially over the course of my career. I believe this organization is on the cusp of significant growth. I'd love to be shoulder to shoulder with you in expanding your reach."

- "It seems like this organization is our city's best-kept secret. I'm a storyteller. I know how to spread good ideas through public relations and free media. I can help you with that."

Put some thought into how you envision using your experience, knowledge, and skills in the boardroom. Show them that you're ready to use this expertise. Sharing your personal impact hypothesis positions you as a *doer* who's eager to partner with leadership in appropriate ways to strengthen the work.

Discuss Board Member Expectations

Nonprofits sometimes fail to clearly communicate the full range of responsibilities expected of every board member. Perhaps they're so eager to add a new director that they soft-pedal the expectations in these early conversations so as to not scare the candidate away. That's a mistake. It's better for a candidate to know the full slate of responsibilities *before* joining the board. The worst-case scenario is for a new board member to learn about the expectations *after* they've been elected and experience the governance equivalent of "buyer's remorse."

I place this responsibility squarely on both parties to get it right. The nonprofit leaders you meet should be clear with you about board member expectations from the outset. The best way to do this is for the organization to provide every candidate with a written document that formally outlines board member roles and responsibilities. This is sometimes referred to as a "board member job description." As a potential board candidate, if they don't offer this document to you in the first meeting, ask for it. If they don't have one already, it's not unreasonable to ask if it would be possible for the expectations to be documented in writing for clarity's sake. You likely wouldn't accept a new job without first seeing the position description. Likewise, you shouldn't accept a board role without understanding what will be expected of you.

Check In on Chemistry and Agree on Next Steps

Before the end of the meeting, try to get a sense of how they're feeling about your potential candidacy, and then talk about next steps. If you have any areas of concern about your fit for the board, don't keep them a secret. Transparency and candor are important qualities in the board development process.

Agree on who will take the next step. If a follow-up process hasn't been mentioned, as a candidate, it's okay to ask: *Is there anything you need from me? Is there somebody else in the organization I should meet with next?*

You might also ask about the organization's time frame for making a decision, but be prepared for a slow-moving process. I once had a candidate say to me after his first meeting with the nonprofit's leadership, "I don't think they're interested in me, so I think I'll pull myself from consideration. I'm just not feeling the love." When I inquired as to why he had that impression, he explained that when he goes through job interview processes, he's rather used to being wined-and-dined, including receiving fast turnaround on communication and decisions.

That's a great approach when hiring a superstar, but it's frequently not possible in nonprofit board development. Why? Well, remember that, by design, nonprofit organizations have a diffuse leadership structure. As it relates to building the board, no one person has singular decision-making power. Oftentimes, a host of people will need to be consulted at various stages of the process.

The nonprofit board development process typically involves a number of consecutive steps, but if you've seen one board development process, you've seen one board development process. Every organization has designed one that works for them. Here's just one example:

- Candidate has a first meeting with the chief executive. *If that goes well and both agree to move forward, then …*

- Candidate meets with one or more members of a nominating committee. *If that goes well, then …*

- Candidate is invited to participate in a site visit. *If that goes well, then …*

- Candidate meets with the board chair and/or the executive committee. *If that goes well, then …*

- Candidate is presented to the full board of directors for nomination, and after a formal and favorable vote …

- Candidate is elected to the board.

After each step, there's a delay in time. Sometimes, this is simply a matter of waiting for the next committee or board meeting so that the matter can be brought up as an agenda item. Other times, the delay is due to scheduling challenges given the busy calendars of those involved in the process.

Don't be frustrated if it feels like your candidacy has stalled. Delay does not equate to disinterest in board development. It's usually driven by adherence to a process.

As a candidate, however, my recommendation is to do the opposite of what the board does. You're a committee of one, if you will, so the delays you cause won't be as easy to understand. Demonstrate your enthusiasm with quick responses. After the first meeting, send a thank-you note, just like you would in a job search. When they reach out to you about next steps, respond right away and make yourself available as soon as possible. Don't offer dates that are weeks or months down the road. Instead, clear your calendar as best you can, demonstrating your eagerness to keep the process moving forward.

I once had a nonprofit walk away from a senior executive as a candidate for their board because he couldn't make himself available for weeks on end. The nonprofit's executive director explained her decision: "He seems great, but if it's *this* hard to get on his calendar at *this* stage of the process, it won't be any easier when we're trying to schedule board and committee meetings that involve many more calendars than just his." Touché—point taken.

Visit the Site

Make one of your touchpoints during the vetting stage a visit to the organization's physical space, whether that's a school, a theater, a clinic, a shelter, a community center, a warehouse, or something else. By seeing the program in action, you'll learn a great deal about the nonprofit. You'll get a front-row seat to staff morale and culture, and you'll see how the organization interacts with its beneficiaries. Take the time to get to know the team members you meet. Hear directly from program beneficiaries what they most appreciate about the organization. Get a feel for how the nonprofit's values show up in the day-to-day work.

A site visit is useful even when there isn't a formal program space. A policy organization, for example, probably won't have much more than offices and conference rooms to see. There likely won't be clients hanging around either. You'll still find value in meeting team members and getting a feel for the office vibe.

By taking time out of your busy day for a site visit, you'll send a powerful message to the organization about your interest. These memorable experiences can help a board candidate cement their interest as they witness the impact being made through the daily work.

Now, Decisions Must Be Made

You've learned a great deal about your target organization and what board service involves, and now it's time to decide if this is a marriage made in heaven. The organization has a decision to make, as well, in that nominating committees often vet more candidates than they have room for on their board in an upcoming round of elections.

Assuming all parties are ready to move forward, your name will be added to a slate of board candidates to be elected at an upcoming board meeting. If you decide against standing for election at any stage in the process described previously, there's one important rule that you must follow: Do not "ghost" the organization! This may seem obvious, but you'd be surprised how often consummate professionals simply go missing when the nonprofit's leadership is trying to communicate with them about next steps in the process. Have the hard conversation. Be direct. Explain to the nonprofit's leadership why you've decided to pull yourself from consideration. In doing so, you can walk away proud of the way you handled yourself. Moreover, you've likely given them helpful information they can use to strengthen the board opportunity for others in the future. A particularly gracious approach is to share that you plan to be a friend and donor to the organization, even though you won't be serving on the board.

If the organization decides against inviting you to stand for nomination at some point in the process, the hard conversation falls on them. Unfortunately, many nonprofit leaders are reluctant to speak candidly with candidates about why they've decided to move in another direction. It's no fun to disappoint people, and, of course, in this case the person being let down is someone volunteering to provide leadership and support.

You can encourage candor by explicitly inviting transparent feedback. "I know there are lots of reasons why the board could have decided that I'm not the right fit. I'd really appreciate it if you could share how that conversation went. I promise there will be no hard feelings either way. I'm eager to learn from this experience."

One of the trickiest conversations for a nonprofit's leader to have is when the candidate's personal identity doesn't sync up with the board's needs. Board diversity should always be a high priority for nonprofit organizations. In board development processes, it's vital that organizations ensure that a wide array of backgrounds, experiences, and perspectives are represented on the board of directors. This often means that boards are factoring in the diversity of the board as it relates to gender and gender identity, race and ethnicity, sexual orientation, disability status, veteran status, and age, among other characteristics. As a candidate, seek to understand the board's perspective in making this decision, even when it might lead to personal disappointment. Communicate that you, too, value diversity and honor that the organization holds it as an important value.

What's Next?

"Do I *really* need to follow this guide in the first meeting and vetting process?" My answer is a resounding, "Yes!" Why? Because it will give you a significant advantage. Candidates who don't show up prepared in this way won't shine in the same way you will.

In my role as board chair of Broadway Inspirational Voices (BIV), the organization's executive director, Angela Grovey, and I interviewed a board candidate who worked at a prominent global professional services firm. To be blunt, he did everything wrong. He didn't seem to know anything about our history or our service to the community, telegraphing that he'd engaged in virtually no research prior to the meeting. When we asked about his interest in joining the board, he struggled to articulate anything more than, "I love Broadway!" He wrapped up by asking Angela—our exceptional and tireless leader who often shoulders an overwhelming workload—to send information that was easily available to him on our website. After the meeting, Angela and I agreed in a thirty-second conversation that there was no need to advance him to the next step in our vetting process.

Preparation matters. Professionalism matters. Demonstrating your enthusiasm matters. Explaining your *why* matters. Showing up with a high level of curiosity matters.

A huge part of the joy and satisfaction we get in our work at Cause Strategy Partners comes in the form of feedback from the nonprofit leaders we're privileged to serve in board development. After they meet our BoardLead candidates, they often say something like, "Wow, the candidate you introduced us to was so prepared!" or "Your candidate nearly had me in tears as they described their connection to our mission!" or "I've never had a candidate ask better questions!" I never tire of hearing it. Setting our candidates up for this kind of success is part of the BoardLead secret sauce. I hope you'll avail yourself of the guidance in this chapter as you step into your first meeting as a board candidate and move through the vetting process. It has a track record of real success!

Reflection Questions

- Do you lean in the direction of joining a smaller board or larger board? Why?

- What is your personal impact hypothesis for the organization you'll meet with?

- Which questions will you ask in the first meeting? Have you confirmed that they aren't already answered on the organization's website?

Chapter
Seven

Starting Strong:
Your Good Governance Boot Camp

It is better to be prepared for an opportunity and not have one than to have an opportunity and not be prepared.

—WHITNEY M. YOUNG JR.

Think about a time when you kicked your feet up on the couch, turned on the television, and clicked over to a channel that was in the middle of a movie. Sometimes you come across an old favorite and—even though it's in the middle of a story—you stay tuned in. I'm pretty sure I've dropped in on *The Godfather* about seventeen times midstream and stayed.

But consider those times when you've sat down for a movie that's somewhere in the middle of the story and it's a *new* movie to you. You have a problem when you make that choice, don't you? You don't know the characters or their arcs. You don't know what has happened in the story to get the plot to where it currently is. You don't know the conflict that has happened in the past. You don't know the driving force of the protagonist—that thing they will stop at nothing to accomplish, no matter the hurdles put in their way.

Tony Award–winning director, Michael Blakemore, wrote, "When the curtain goes up, the audience is in trouble."[13] Why? Because theatergoers enter into a story and need to quickly sort out what's going on.

Joining a nonprofit board is a lot like dropping into the middle of a movie or sitting down for a show as the curtain rises. There are key players you need to get to know, several driving forces to understand, and an organizational history that influences decision-making today. There are third rails you don't want to touch, and there are past organizational experiences your fellow board members will bring up without context. Board and staff members will use a host of acronyms you've never heard before, and programmatic features will be discussed that you don't yet know. There will be challenges they didn't tell you about during your board interviews, and the organization may have more dysfunction than you'd expected, lingering somewhere below the surface.

Given this complex context of unknowns, where do you begin? Let's set you up with guidance for how you should be thinking and behaving as you begin your term on a nonprofit board.

Review Key Information Provided to New Board Members to Understand the Operating Context

An effective onboarding program includes providing new board members with a comprehensive board handbook, often delivered in virtual form today. These materials, taken as a whole, will help a new board member learn the structure within which governance operates

---

13   Jack Viertel, The Secret Life of the American Musical: How Broadway Shows Are Built (New York City: Sarah Crichton Books, 2016), 18.

and begin to understand the internal and external landscapes. These resources will also serve as an ongoing point of reference throughout one's tenure on the board. The following checklist provides a thorough list of the materials new board members should receive and review as they begin to serve.

Information about the organization

- A recent annual report
- Promotional materials (e.g., brochures, newsletters, a press kit)
- Published media stories and recent press releases

Board materials

- Board member role and responsibilities document
- Board roster with contact information
- Calendar of scheduled meetings and other activities to attend
- Board committee list and committee charters
- Bylaws
- Proof of directors and officers insurance
- Meeting minutes (documenting the most recent board meetings)

Information about staff, finances, and strategy

- Organizational chart (list of staff and positions)
- Written strategic plan or strategic framework
- Financials (most recent financial report presented to the board)
- Form 990 (most recent completed fiscal year)
- Audit (most recent completed fiscal year)

Use the Strategic Framework as a Guidepost for Your Board Service

Remember that a core responsibility of board service is to shape the strategic direction of the organization. The organization's strategy serves as a compass, guiding and aligning resources, activities, and decisions with the organization's long-term vision and near-term growth plan. As a new board member, you should commit the high-level objectives of the organization's strategy to memory and frame your thinking, decision-making, comments, and questions at board meetings around those priorities.

I once surprised the members of a nonprofit board with a pop quiz a few months after we had collectively completed a robust strategic planning process. During a board meeting, I asked the directors to name the four top-line strategic objectives in the newly minted plan. The results, unfortunately, were *not pretty* as board members struggled to articulate our core strategic goals. After repeating the pop quiz a couple more times in future meetings, these four priorities eventually became internalized by board members and helped ensure their board service remained purposeful and aligned with intended goals.

What if your organization doesn't have a written strategy in place? Become a leading voice on the board advocating for a planning process. Strategic frameworks clarify purpose, define future objectives, ensure the alignment of efforts, provide guidance on resource allocation, and serve as a powerful communication tool for a full range of stakeholder groups.

Participate in Boardroom Conversations by Asking Great Questions, Sharing Your Perspectives, and Staying Flexible

Every board member's personal insight and experience are important and useful. Don't be afraid to chime in, even as a new board member. Your fresh eyes on a problem may be just the perspective the organization needs. At the same time, remember that you have a lot to learn, so listen more than you talk as you get started on the board.

Keep in mind that you are one voice among many. In board decision-making, the perspectives of a range of stakeholders should be factored in: your fellow board members, community members, staff members, clients, and funders, for example. It's good to have a point of view while at the same time staying open; an even better idea may be just around the corner. I don't know who said this first, but it is a good rule of thumb in nonprofit governance: Board members should have a perspective, but not an agenda.

Know Your Three Legal Duties

The moment you're elected to a board, three legal duties attach themselves to you. On the day your name shows up on the meeting minutes and throughout your tenure on the board, you're expected to fulfill specific legal requirements. In my experience, the degree to which board members are aware of their three legal duties varies greatly. While some board members may generally be aware of these responsibilities, it's safe to say that many would be unable to name even one of their three legal duties, much less articulate an operable understanding of what they require.

As both a lawyer and a champion of good governance in the nonprofit sector, I feel strongly that every new board member should have, at the very least, a preliminary understanding of their three legal duties: the duty of care, the duty of obedience, and the duty of loyalty. Being aware of these legal duties will help ensure that you don't unintentionally breach your fiduciary responsibilities or find yourself facing unwanted legal consequences. Acting consistently with these duties helps protect you, your nonprofit's interests, and the organization's credibility in the community.

Knowing what the law requires of governing board members is an important part of starting strong. Given my legal background, this topic is close to my heart, but I fully recognize that others—and perhaps you—might find it less compelling. I'll keep this boring-but-important information brief, I promise. Even so, as you continue your board service journey, I strongly encourage you and your fellow board members to pursue continuing educational opportunities that will give you a more comprehensive understanding of each one of these important obligations.

Duty of Care

The duty of care requires individuals to act responsibly as they govern, shepherd, and guide the nonprofit organization they serve as a member of the board of directors. What does it look like to "act responsibly" in this way? The legal answer is one that only a lawyer can love: *to exercise the same amount of care a reasonably prudent person would use under similar circumstances in managing the affairs of the organization.* But what does that mean in practice? If you attend meetings regularly, review board meeting materials, stay up to date on what's happening in the organization, and make thoughtful, independent, and well-informed decisions, you'll meet your duty of care.

One aspect of meeting the duty of care that can feel daunting for many new board members is the financial oversight role. This responsibility can create anxiety because it involves diving into the waters of financial management, which, for many, is well outside of their core knowledge and skill set. This may hold true even for people with a finance background. There are similarities in financial management between the for-profit and the nonprofit sectors, including basic financial principles such as budgeting, reporting, accounting, and establishing financial controls. There are, however, important differences to keep in mind, as well.

One fundamental difference is the centrality of the profit motive. For-profit entities are organized to generate profits for shareholders. Responsible companies have additional motivations, as well, including looking out for the interests of other stakeholder groups: customers, employees, the community, and more. But ultimately, a business's profit motive is of central importance. A nonprofit organization's focus, on the other hand, relates to mission accomplishment. Nonprofits should finish with monetary surpluses most years, of course, in order to remain financially sustainable for the long haul, but those surpluses stay within the organization to advance its core purpose. Other differences in nonprofit financial oversight relate to required reporting standards for nonprofits, specific regulatory requirements for tax-exempt organizations, and the importance of the diversity of revenue sources that fuel the work.

To perform your financial oversight role well and ensure that you meet the duty of care, you'll want to familiarize yourself with five key financial reports and documents. One is the Form 990, which we covered in detail in chapter 3. Here are the other four:

- *The Budget:* A financial plan, approved by the board, that provides detail on the money the organization expects to receive (revenue) and how that money will be spent (expenses) over the course of the fiscal year.

- *The P&L Statement*: A financial report that shows the revenue generated and the expenses incurred over a specific period. When compared side-by-side with the budget, a board member can better understand the organization's overall financial performance as compared to the plan.

- *The Balance Sheet:* A financial snapshot—based on a specific date—that shows what the organization owns (assets), what it owes (liabilities), and what remains (equity), as of that date.

- *The Audit:* A thorough review of an organization's financial records, transactions, and accounts conducted by an independent auditor or accounting firm in order to validate accuracy and ensure conformity with accounting standards.

Organizations may or may not be required to perform an annual audit depending on state and federal regulations, the size of the organization, the amount of annual revenue, its funding sources, and other factors.

It should be noted that there are other financial reports that help a board member perform the financial oversight role well. As a new board member grows in understanding the financial reports, they will be able to offer more value to the organization and further strengthen their performance as it relates to the duty of care.

Duty of Obedience

The duty of obedience requires board members to act in faithfulness to the mission of the organization, as described in the organization's foundational documents such as the nonprofit's Articles of Incorporation and Bylaws. The board of directors must always act in ways and make decisions that align with and advance the organization's stated purpose. Seems simple, right? For the most part, it is. But board members should nonetheless remain vigilant.

The severe financial downturn that resulted as the U.S. housing market bubble burst in 2008 had widespread repercussions on the global economy. The subprime mortgage crisis had a negative financial impact on most individuals and organizations, including the nonprofit organization I was leading at the time, CGLA. Philanthropic and charitable giving declined or dried up from virtually every revenue source, including private foundations, individuals, and corporations. As I received notice after notice from key funders that their giving to CGLA would be sliced dramatically, I realized that we were in real trouble.

I quickly engaged the organization's board of directors in a strategic conversation to figure out how to respond to the significant and certain shortfall in revenue we would soon face. One board member shared an idea in that meeting:

> *What if we offer our legal services to the community on a sliding scale? For example, our clients who are living below the poverty rate would continue to receive our services for free, but those who could pay would be charged fees based on a sliding scale, all the way up to market rate. Our staff attorneys are first-rate lawyers. There is a market for these services and it would help us bring in much-needed revenue to weather this storm.*

Was this an innovative idea for generating additional revenue to keep CGLA's doors open during a challenging financial crisis? Absolutely. The problem was that our mission statement was very clear about whom we existed to serve—"individuals and families living in poverty." More than one of our thoughtful board members noted that such a decision would amount to mission creep and would almost certainly violate the board's duty of obedience. They were right to speak up, and the idea was immediately dropped.

Duty of Loyalty

The duty of loyalty requires board members to always act in the best interests of the organization and, specifically, to prioritize the organization's interests above self-interest. An important aspect of this duty is the responsibility of a board member to disclose potential conflicts of interest. Think of potential conflicts as competing interests that could influence one's decision-making, impacting their judgment and objectivity. In nonprofit governance, conflicts of interest sometimes show up in the form of potential financial benefits that could flow to a board member or someone close to them. When a board member has a potential conflict, they have the responsibility to disclose it to the board, to remove themselves from deliberations, and to allow the independent, or nonconflicted, members of the board to determine whether or not the transaction is nonetheless in the best interests of the organization. In short, board members are fiduciaries and must not leverage their position on the board for personal gain or to benefit others at the expense of the organization.

I served on the board of an organization with a board member who was an attorney specializing in nonprofit law. Every year, the organization was required to file certain legal documents to meet administrative requirements. This board member would offer to provide these legal services to the organization at 50 percent of the market rate. He viewed this deeply discounted service as another way to contribute to the organization. To be clear, under this arrangement, he would benefit financially from the transaction. The organization would be invoiced by the board member for these services. Even so, this arrangement appeared to be beneficial for the organization, which would save money on legal fees. Each year, before being retained to provide these services, this board member would disclose his offer. He would then be asked to step out of the room, while the remaining nonconflicted directors discussed whether the transaction was in the best interests of the organization. Given the steep discount, the board always approved the arrangement and expressed appreciation for his kind offer.

While it may seem obvious that the offer was in the best interests of the organization, it was nonetheless very important for the board member to disclose the potential conflict and not participate in the board discussion or determination. Liberally disclosing potential conflicts as a board member and following this protocol help remove any whiff of impropriety.

Another aspect of this duty is the expectation that board members maintain confidentiality about board proceedings. By failing to meet this expectation, a board member potentially puts the organization's reputation at risk or creates an environment that can lead to the loss of trust among stakeholders.

This responsibility requires personal integrity and discipline, particularly when controversial decisions are made by the board and the public or key stakeholders of the organization ask for—or even demand—an explanation. It may ultimately be in the best interests of the organization to share details of the decision-making process, demonstrating the important values of transparency and account-ability. That is for the board to decide as a collective. Even so, each board member has an individual duty to maintain confidentiality around board proceedings. A board's collective effort at striking the right balance between transparency and confidentiality on sensitive matters is, in my view, part of the fine art of governance.

Understanding Management versus Board Responsibility

By design, the board of directors and the chief executive share lead-ership of the organization. As I've discussed, the board is charged with setting strategy, driving resources, providing fiduciary oversight, and championing functional area excellence in their areas of profes-sional expertise. Acting in parallel, the chief executive has a long list of responsibilities as well, from making day-to-day management and operational decisions to fundraising to managing the work of the staff to cultivating relationships with a host of stakeholders. I've seen nonprofit CEO job descriptions that are pages and pages long. By the end of reading them, one might fairly conclude that only a fantastical superhero could possibly live up to the role's expectations. Yet despite the litany of articulated responsibilities, a nonprofit chief executive's core role can be boiled down to one overarching charge: to successfully execute the mission of the organization consistent with the strategic objectives articulated by the board of directors.

An important issue that often comes up in governance relates to the question of who gets to make a particular decision. Recall that nonprofits operate with a complex leadership structure designed to ensure that no one person has concentrated, independent power. This means that it can be difficult—on any number of issues—to know whether an issue should be decided by the board of directors or whether it's appropriate for autonomous management decision-making by the CEO. Getting these judgment calls right is another aspect of the fine art of nonprofit leadership.

It's easy to understand why a board might want to engage on as many organizational issues as possible. Their passion for the mission leads them to care deeply about the ins and outs of how the work is done. Before long, they can end up in the weeds. Directors walk into the boardroom with business prowess; their professional skills are leveraged daily at work. They can forget that governance is a legislative, rather than executive, function. It's also natural for board members to focus their attention on the things they know best rather than the more challenging and intimidating aspects of nonprofit board service like fundraising, ambassadorship, and board development.

Here's rule number one: Don't become a micromanaging board member. Rule number two? Don't let your board become a group of micromanagers either. Keep in mind that it's the chief executive who is most negatively impacted by a micromanaging board. They can become frustrated, dispirited, and exhausted when a micromanaging board crosses the management-board divide and engages in the wrong way and on the wrong things.

So, how can an organization prevent this from happening? Given that the dividing line between governance and management is often gray, how should each leadership entity understand its decision-making responsibilities?

I encourage chief executives to take the temperature of the board as a collective. How engaged in discussion and decision-making do they expect to be? I've seen boards that run the full gamut. In general, boards will engage on the matters the chief executive puts in front of them and will stay out of the things they don't. The chief executive should choose the topics to be surfaced with the board wisely. I've watched nonprofit chief executives share with their boards the full litany of things they're dealing with, only to have it backfire. What starts as an intention to impress "the bosses" with how hard they're working soon turns into frustration when they discover that board members have opinions on all manner of items, big and small. When a chief executive opens the door for discussion on what is a management- or staff-level issue, they shouldn't be surprised when board members walk right in, viewing it as an invitation to opine.

In addition, the chief executive and the board chair should discuss what constitutes a board-level versus a management-level decision. The board chair might give examples of matters that were properly raised with the board rather than handled independently by management. The chief executive could provide a handful of examples of matters that, in their view, wouldn't require board involvement, checking in on alignment with the board chair. Ultimately, both parties should agree that judgment calls will have to be made by the chief executive on a regular basis. With this understanding in mind, the board chair should do their best to support the chief executive and provide assurance. The message is "I've got your back."

Even with this foundation in place, however, expect issues to surface that will lead you to think to yourself, "Is this the board's decision or the chief executive's decision?" My hope is that *you* will be the board member who asks that question out loud—even early in your tenure.

But how does leadership get to the right answer? Here's my best advice for arriving at the proper resolution when trying to figure out if a decision belongs to the board or to the chief executive.

A Guide for Deciding Who Decides: Management or Board?

As a first step, read the bylaws. Oftentimes, this foundational document will articulate specific issues and circumstances when the board must be involved. The bylaws might, for example, require a board action for a contractual obligation or expenditure over a certain amount of money. Chief executives and board members alike must carefully follow the framework set out in the bylaws.

In practice, however, most of the time the bylaws won't tell you which party decides a discrete issue. To figure it out, I offer seven principles for board members and chief executives to apply when deciding whether a matter should be surfaced with the board for discussion and a decision:

1. *Permanence:* The longer the decision's implications will stay with the organization, the more likely the matter should be raised with the board. Take, for example, a twenty-year lease of new office space or sunsetting one of the organization's programs.

2. *Controversial:* The more contentious the decision is with one or more stakeholder groups, the more likely the matter should be raised with the board. The board of directors is more likely to have the chief executive's back after an outcry ignites if they've participated in the deliberations and final decision.

3. *Complex:* Some issues fall outside the expertise of the chief executive and would benefit from the diverse perspectives, wisdom, knowledge, and skill sets represented on the board.

4. *Positional:* Consider whether the issue at hand involves having the organization take a public stand. The board may need to be involved when the organization places a stake in the ground on a policy issue, signs an open letter to a public official, or advocates for new legislation. The position may not feel controversial from the chief executive's vantage point, but if it will have the imprimatur of the organization on it, chances are that the decision should be informed by the board.

5. *Essential:* The board owns the mission, vision, and values of the organization. A chief executive must not fiddle with these core essentials of the organization without full board involvement.

6. *Directional:* The more closely related the decision is to the strategic direction of the organization, the more likely the matter should be raised with the board. Remember, shaping strategy is a shared responsibility of the chief executive and the board. Chief executives must not go it alone.

7. *Financial:* The board establishes an annual budget to provide management with the autonomy needed to make day-to-day financial decisions. The board then regularly tracks outcomes against the budget over the course of the year through financial reporting. Although we certainly don't want boards approving routine expenses or expecting consultation for minor budgetary adjustments, when a significant departure from the budget is anticipated, the board should be involved.

When the board and CEO find the sweet spot between proper board engagement and effective management execution, leaders are happy, organizations are well-run, and the mission is much more likely to be achieved.

Seven Archetypes of a Great Board Member

As you begin to serve, you'll discover a range of different approaches to board service as you observe your fellow board members. These board service styles will likely be as diverse as the board members themselves. Individuals tap into their unique leadership strengths—and yes, often-times their personal idiosyncrasies, as well—as they govern nonprofit organizations alongside their board colleagues.

After years of observing countless board members in action, I've identified seven board member archetypes that are particularly effective. Each one brings a set of characteristics that combine to produce a highly impactful board leader. A few focus mostly on adding internal value to the organization or board. Others home in on driving value with external stakeholders. Some are a nice balance of the two. These seven archetypes are organized in the following pages by starting with those that mostly have an internal focus, and proceeding to those focused primarily on external impact.

A word of warning: It's sometimes said that every strength has a dark side. The positive attributes of each archetype can have a risk point, as well. A wonderful characteristic, handled in an unskillful way, can be, at best, unhelpful and, at worst, a significant liability. With that in mind, try each one of these archetypes on for size. Perhaps one or two will help you develop a plan for driving impact as a board member in ways that leverage your personal strengths. Which one is best suited for you?

THE TRUSTED ADVISOR: AVAILABLE. HONEST. RELIABLE.

You've heard the saying, "Leadership is lonely." It's true. It really is. A nonprofit chief executive is the one individual in most organizations without a peer. Board members have their fellow board members, and staff members have their colleagues. The chief executive sits between the two groups alone, a position that can feel isolating.

A board member in the Trusted Advisor role understands that leadership can be isolating so that they form a special relationship with the chief executive. They invest a significant amount of time with the CEO outside of the boardroom, building rapport and trust. They serve as a confidant and mentor. They offer to serve as a sounding board, providing a safe space for the chief executive to express frustration, share concerns, or test ideas. The Trusted Advisor provides encouragement, of course, but also artfully provides private and candid feedback when the chief executive has missed the mark.

One of my board members, Jeremy Taylor, was a Trusted Advisor to me. He often invited me to Chicago Cubs games at Wrigley Field. We regularly had lunch at Weber Grill Restaurant downtown. We checked in on the phone from time to time. With this intentionally built friendship, Jeremy was well positioned to provide me with not only positive encouragement, of course, but also tough feedback. He could offer guidance on difficult issues without holding back because trust was firmly in place. Jeremy would often call me while I was driving home from a board meeting, just to check in. "How are you feeling about how that went?"

The Trusted Advisor can play an important role in strengthening the well-being, engagement, and overall performance of the CEO. A risk point, however, is that the friendship formed between the two can unintentionally lead to an imbalance in influence vis-à-vis other board members. The special relationship might also make it more difficult for this board member to act against the interests of the CEO, even when it becomes necessary to do so as a fiduciary of the organization.

THE TECHNICAL EXPERT: SKILLED. WILLING. ACCESSIBLE.

Lisa Dietlin is a fundraising expert who created a consultancy many years ago, called The Institute of Transformational Philanthropy. As a board member, she delivered her expertise to the nonprofit she served, chairing the Development Committee, helping shape fundraising strategy, and serving as a critical thought partner to the executive director and director of development. In very practical ways, Lisa provided tangible value that would have cost tens of thousands of dollars to secure from a consultant, but as a board member, she delivered it all pro bono. Lisa knew her sweet spot and offered it generously as a board leader to drive impact.

Nonprofit chief executives are asked to be all things to all people. Want evidence? Visit www.idealist.org and look through active executive director or CEO job postings. The list of responsibilities, qualifications, and desired personal competencies is extensive. In fact, I'm pretty confident that an all-powerful deity would fall short of meeting the expectations articulated in most nonprofit leadership position descriptions. Given this reality, a nonprofit leader is bolstered when they partner with technical experts on their board, particularly in functional areas that are less familiar.

Board members often bring professional expertise in one or more skill sets that they can contribute to the organization in meaningful ways. The Technical Expert leverages their professional skills to bring about results. They act as an issue spotter, quality assurance provider, and sounding board on areas within their zone of mastery. They serve as a thought partner on functional areas in their wheelhouse. They identify needed consulting engagements, help develop a scope of work, and tap their professional network to source experts who might provide pro bono assistance. Remaining vigilant about appropriate divisions in board and management responsibilities, the Technical Expert helps the organization build capacity in their area of core competency, whether that's strategy, people operations, marketing, legal, real estate, technology, or another capability.

A risk point for technical experts is micromanagement. Simply out of enthusiasm for the work and the opportunity to deliver their expertise, this board member runs the risk of overstepping the board's responsibility and engaging in work that properly rests with the chief executive and staff. They can find it challenging to not be operators. In addition, there's the risk that the Technical Expert will focus too much attention on their area of specialized knowledge and, in doing so, will fail to keep in view the broad strategic perspective that is part and parcel of governance.

THE MISSION GUARDIAN: DEDICATED. PURPOSEFUL. KNOWLEDGEABLE.

This board member possesses a strong sense of purpose and a keen understanding of the nonprofit's history, context, and founding intentions. The Mission Guardian is highly attuned to the potential risks of mission drift or deviation from the nonprofit's core values and objectives. They serve as the conscience of the organization, ensuring that the nonprofit remains true to its foundational principles in all endeavors.

Very often, this individual has served on the board for some time, perhaps since the early years of the organization's existence. They may have had a close relationship with the founder and participated in the group's early growth. The Mission Guardian feels a personal responsibility to remind those associated with the organization of not just what they can *become* but of where they have *come from*. They often focus their contributions in meetings on how the past has shaped the success of the organization.

Recall Broadway Inspirational Voices (BIV), a Tony Award-honored gospel choir composed of a diverse array of Broadway artists founded by Michael McElroy in 1994. McElroy's original purpose in creating BIV was to bring hope and inspiration to the Broadway community, which, at the time, was being decimated by the impact of the HIV-AIDS crisis. Having grown up in the black church, McElroy knew firsthand the power of gospel music to provide emotional support and spiritual healing to a hurting world. John Eric Parker, an original BIV choir member, now serves as a member of the board of directors. He embodies the original values of the choir and is well positioned to safeguard its core purpose. John Eric helps the board shape the future growth of the organization in ways that reflect McElroy's original vision and the organization's core strengths: its remarkable heritage, its reason for being, and the values that guided BIV from the start.

The Mission Guardian has risk points, as well. They must avoid being unnecessarily resistant to change. A rigid view of the past could lead them to overemphasize the organization's historical roots rather than support growth and development. Such inflexibility might lead to missed opportunities, debilitating conflict with staff and fellow board members, or the risk of becoming less relevant to important stakeholder groups as society evolves.

When the Mission Guardian maintains an open mind while also championing the organization's roots, they play an important role in protecting the *heart and soul* of the organization while simultaneously encouraging growth. Their viewpoint likely represents a large swath of the organization's stakeholders—longtime donors, loyal staff members, and long-serving volunteers. The importance of the Mission Guardian's commitment to preserving the nonprofit's identity and purpose should not be underestimated.

THE PENSIVE SAGE: REFLECTIVE. THOUGHTFUL. RESPECTED.

In board meetings, Dan Wilkening—a senior executive at a major financial institution—would sit quietly for the lion's share of the meeting. He would lean back in his chair, listen carefully, take notes and nod occasionally, but rarely speak. As a well-respected executive, Dan's deference during board conversations was initially surprising to me. Over time, however, I learned to see Dan's approach as a great strength and, in fact, coined a phrase for it in my head: *The Wilkening Effect.* When we were at the crossroads of a complex or contentious discussion on an important strategic issue, Dan would eventually lean forward in his seat, put his elbows on the table, lift an index finger, and wait to be invited by the chairperson to jump into the conversation. When Dan spoke, his colleagues listened. Thereafter, the discussion would usually begin to move in the direction of Dan's carefully considered position.

The Pensive Sage listens more than they speak. They look for ways to think about issues differently. They ask great questions to ensure thoughtful debate. And when they make a point, it counts. They embody a blend of thoughtful introspection, wisdom gained from experience, and a penchant for sharing insightful perspectives pulled from a deep well of knowledge and experience.

With that said, the Pensive Sage should be careful to avoid being overly introspective, forcing lengthy deliberation on an issue that leads to paralysis in decision-making. Board meeting agendas are often designed to cover a great deal of ground in a limited amount of time. The Pensive Sage must guard against being so reflective that the organization fails to take timely action on important decisions.

Furthermore, as individuals who may have a great deal of gravitas vis-à-vis fellow board members, the Pensive Sage should work hard to build meaningful and authentic relationships with colleagues, demonstrating high levels of respect for others and encouraging inclusive participation. A dynamic in which others regularly defer to a more senior board member's perspective, almost by default, is not a set up for healthy governance.

THE OPPORTUNITY SEEKER: ENTHUSIASTIC. ENTERPRISING. CREATIVE.

After listening to the executive director's report at a board meeting and learning that staff morale was in decline, board member Adam Stanley (mentioned in chapter 4) spoke up. Looking around the room at his colleagues, he said, "There is something we can do to help." Adam spent the next few weeks rallying board members to hold a Staff Appreciation Day for the dedicated but dispirited team. He gathered dozens of donated gifts from his fellow board members, including tickets to sporting events and concerts, airline miles, artwork, gift certificates, and more. He then organized a celebratory party and asked board members to prepare words of praise for each staff member. On the day of the event, a chartered bus picked the staff up for a tour of the city, while the board transitioned the drab office space into a party setting. When the bus returned, staff members entered the office to a New Orleans–style band playing "When the Saints Go Marching In" as board members stood on both sides of a rolled-out red carpet, cheering and applauding the team. Thanks to just one board member, a staff on the edge of burnout experienced a sense of joy and rejuvenation, having been seen and appreciated by the organization's governing board.

The Opportunity Seeker has a proactive mindset and a keen eye for identifying needs and getting things done. They're naturally inclined to look for new opportunities and unlock initiatives that align with the organization's mission. Highly enthusiastic and forward-thinking, the Opportunity Seeker looks for problems to solve and then acts. They're eager to apply their time, talent, and treasure to advance the organization without putting an extra burden on the chief executive or staff members. In fact, they lift burdens off of the team and make them their own.

Taking a page from Adam Stanley and his Staff Appreciation Day, I recently threw a pizza party for the staff members of Nonprofit New York. My intention was to thank the staff for their hard work in executing a successful citywide conference. Realizing that this might also be an opportunity to build connections with a number of new staff members I hadn't yet had the opportunity to meet, I took along a set of question cards designed to help people learn more about one another.

This hour-and-a-half-long lunch turned into a deeply meaningful experience for everyone. As staff members shared at a personal and sometimes rather deep level, spirits were lifted, and stronger relationships were forged. At the end of our time together, I was able to express to the staff how much we, as board members, appreciate them for their work and how we admire their collective talents as they execute the aims of the organization. Unlike the extensive commitment Adam Stanley made, my extra effort required just $175 and a couple of hours of time. The value of the experience far surpassed the investment.

Is there a risk point for the Opportunity Seeker? You bet. This board member's enthusiasm might cause them to take on too much, pushing themselves—and maybe even the entire board—beyond their limits. It's important that the Opportunity Seeker carefully assess their capacity before making commitments to engage in ways that exceed the standard expectations of board service. Beginning initiatives without proper follow-through leads to unfinished work—a waste of resources in an always resource-constrained environment. This result can lead to disappointment and undermine trust in the individual board member or the board as a whole.

With that said, the Opportunity Seeker can play a pivotal role in encouraging a culture of forward momentum for the board and within the organization. They identify ways to leverage their personal assets in order to make unique and meaningful contributions. The Opportunity Seeker often contributes more outside the boardroom than they do sitting in a board meeting.

THE PACE SETTER: FULLY ENGAGED. DRIVEN. EXEMPLAR.

Politicians and elected officials sometimes use the phrase "A rising tide lifts all boats" to describe how a growing economy benefits everyone. The aphorism is also helpful in describing the effect of fully engaged board members serving on a nonprofit board. I've seen it over and over again: one or two newly elected high-performing board members take their commitment to drive impact from a board seat seriously and, before long, their colleagues are responding to the upward pressure to become more meaningful contributors themselves. Why is that? Some people simply don't like to be outpaced. Sometimes it's out of respect for the individual's impressive level of involvement. Maybe it's because effective board leadership just needed to be modeled. Occasionally, it's good old-fashioned guilt: "If she's doing that much, I'm embarrassed to do so little."

A Pace Setter can make their mark in a range of ways. Kevin Ryan's first donation as a board member soared well beyond what others on the board had been giving from year to year, leading his colleagues to consider if they might be able to stretch further in their own contribution level. Sylvie Armand's engagement in board meetings set a new standard of participation as she asked thoughtful questions, offered meaningful insights, volunteered for participation on multiple committees, and wondered out loud how else she could add mission value. Soon other board members were elevating their personal level of engagement. Cullen Malley offered to host a meeting at his company's office after joining a board. Every detail was perfect including printed nameplates and welcome gifts preset at every seat around the table, tasty catered food, and first-rate technology (that actually worked!). Existing board members couldn't help but be impressed by this generous contribution from a "newbie." Before long, a fellow board member had followed Cullen's example, offering to host a carefully curated in-person meeting at her employer's headquarters later in the year.

The Pace Setter raises the performance of other board members by setting a high standard of personal engagement, leading by example, and driving momentum toward achieving organizational goals. They shape the culture of the board, embodying a strong work ethic and setting a new benchmark of performance and accountability.

The Pace Setter might make it uncomfortable for others who are less active on the board. To that I say, "Oh well!" This high achiever can leave disengaged colleagues wondering if their own time on the board is winding down as new board members show up with elevated enthusiasm, fresh energy, and a host of new ideas. Frankly, it's hard to view that as a risk point, in my view. The Pace Setter fosters an environment that encourages all board members to stretch themselves and go the extra mile to ensure the success of the organization. For those who are unprepared to meet the standard of full engagement in their board service, this example-based pressure might be just what is needed. Furthermore, disengaged and under-engaged board members sometimes need just this sort of nudge to recognize that it's time to move on.

THE IMPATIENT CATALYST: FORWARD-THINKING. RESTLESS. OPTIMISTIC.

This board member pushes the organization and the chief executive to do more, to do it faster, and to drive greater impact. Their service is characterized by an urgency for change. They're eager to see rapid progress and are proactive about catalyzing transformation within the organization. Sometimes viewed as the "bull in a china shop" by the chief executive or other board members, the Impatient Catalyst pushes for bold initiatives that can lead to transformative outcomes. They're not afraid to challenge the status quo or be perceived as restless, feeling strongly that the organization must adapt quickly in order to thrive in an evolving environment.

Nathan Richardson serves on the Advisory Board of my company. In our first year of operation, he generously offered us no-rent work space in his start-up's trendy SoHo office building, which was outfitted with more desks than they needed at the time. One day while I was typing away on my laptop, Nathan dropped by to check in: "What are you working on?" After sharing details with him about the project that was underway, I added, "The problem is that I'm not finding enough time to do business development." In that conversation and many thereafter, Nathan urged me to get out of the office, meet with potential clients, and focus on growth. "You don't have the luxury to be in the office, Rob. You're building a business. Get out there and make things happen for Cause Strategy Partners."

For nearly a decade, Nathan's board service has been marked by a constant push to think bigger, elevate our profile, increase our pace of growth, and connect with potential partners who might transform the future of our work. As an advisor, Nathan has no personal stake in this work. Rather, the Impatient Catalyst is simply built into his DNA as a person and as a businessman. My firm has benefited greatly as Nathan has brought these attributes to his role on our Advisory Board.

The Impatient Catalyst might demonstrate frustration with bureaucratic processes mired in "Robert's Rules of Order," a historic set of parliamentary procedures designed to ensure efficient and fair decision-making in governance. They become annoyed with slow adaptation to change or resistance to new ideas. Their impatience, however, is usually rooted in a genuine desire to see the organization's mission thrive and build itself for a strong and relevant operation long into the future.

It can sometimes feel like a sense of urgency is missing on nonprofit boards, particularly juxtaposed against for-profit or corporate boards. In my view, this is due in part to motivational forces. Corporate directors generally have a financial stake in the success of the company as shareholders. Increased profits will equal greater financial gains for individual board members. With a self-interested motivation like this absent from nonprofit board service—appropriately so, of course—there may be a lack of inherent drive to push for progress with the necessary urgency. Nonprofit board members, especially newly elected ones, can be reluctant to make others uncomfortable by leaning in and challenging the organization to be more aggressive in pursuing transformation and growth. But when there are one or two board members who take ownership of that responsibility, it can lead to tremendous results.

As with the other archetypes, the Impatient Catalyst has potential risk points to manage, as well. They can be difficult for the chief executive or staff to work with. They must guard against corroding this important relationship, as well as causing unhelpful tension with other board members who prefer a more deliberative approach. While their energy and drive for progress is an organizational asset, it can become a detriment in governance if they insist on hasty decision-making, set unrealistic performance expectations, or generate debilitating conflict in what is often a consensus-based, decision-making environment.

"Having Determined That a Quorum Is Present, This Meeting Is Called to Order"

When the chairman says these words at your first meeting, your board service will be underway. You're now ready to roll! As we have explored in this chapter, you understand that you'll be dropping into the middle of the organization's story and you have a great deal to learn. To position yourself for fast success, you know the materials that you should familiarize yourself with in advance of the first meeting. You'll keep the organization's high-level strategic objectives top of mind, leveraging them in your comments and questions.

As an earnest board member, you'll serve from the outset in a way that reflects your three legal duties: the duties of care, obedience, and loyalty. You'll diligently mind the line between your responsibilities as a board member and the responsibilities that properly belong to the chief executive and their team. When you think the board might be overstepping, you will be the board member who raises their hand and asks for clarification on whether the board or chief executive has the final decision. And as you begin to serve, you'll start carving out your unique approach to board service that drives value to the board and organization. Will you fit squarely into one of the seven archetypes we explored? Or will you develop another approach that makes you uniquely valuable to the mission of the organization?

There's one important area of board service that we haven't yet covered in detail. The time has now come to talk about that usually unfamiliar, often intimidating, sometimes even frightening role that might seem like the most daunting board responsibility for you. It is the "*f*-word" of nonprofit board service. You guessed it: "fundraising."

Acting as a fundraiser for the organization you serve is an important part of starting strong in board service. At Cause Strategy Partners, we're proud to have helped thousands of new board members push through their anxiety to become effective generators of financial support for the causes and organizations they support. Today, our BoardLeaders raise more than $24 million annually for their non-profits, but they began at the same starting point. Fundraising seemed scary and was an activity they'd not tried before. Through our learning experiences, insights, and tools, we've helped countless reluctant, inexperienced, and even terrified professionals become prodigious fundraisers as they stepped into their new identity as a Causie. The next chapter provides guidance on how you can do the same.

Reflection Questions

- Which one of the seven "Archetypes of a Great Board Member" most closely reflects the approach you would like to bring to your board service? How might you lean into that approach to drive greater value more quickly as a new board member?

- Have you memorized the top-line objectives of your organization's strategic framework? List them below. How might these strategic objectives shape your comments and questions in upcoming board meetings?

- Paint the picture of how you will serve as a board member to satisfy your duty of care. Be specific. In the following space, write out your personal commitment describing exactly how you plan to serve your organization from a seat on the board.

Chapter Eight

Demystifying Fundraising for Board Members

Fundraising is the gentle art of inspiring people
to part with something they hold dear.

—HENRY A. ROSSO, FOUNDER, THE
FUND RAISING SCHOOL

"Eric Weng raised $96,680 in his first year serving on the Fiver Children's Foundation board!" a team member yelled out, piercing the hushed environment of our open-concept office space.

"What? No way. That doesn't seem possible," I responded.

"He did! It's right here in his BoardLead one-year impact evaluation."

"Are you sure they didn't mistakenly add an extra zero?" I asked skeptically in reply.

My pessimism wasn't anchored in any lack of confidence about Eric's abilities. I knew firsthand that he was a talented, whip-smart managing director working at an esteemed investment firm. I'd had the opportunity to get to know Eric through his involvement with our BoardLead program. Early on in the process, I phoned Eric to try to talk him into filling an open seat at another nonprofit serving children and youth in the city. After careful consideration, he said,

"Rob, I really love the mission of the Fiver Children's Foundation. If it's alright with you, I'd like to focus my attention there."

Eric had also been an engaged participant in our *BoardLearn Good Governance Boot Camp.* I'd had the opportunity to teach best practices in fundraising to him and his BoardLead cohort, just as they were about to roll onto their boards.

My uncertainty about Eric's reported success in fundraising was simply because he'd served for just one year on Fiver's board. In fact, this was Eric's first time serving on *any* nonprofit board, and it was his first time fundraising for a cause. It was hard for me to believe that he could generate nearly $100,000 so early in his board service journey.

After double-checking with Fiver's executive director, Christie Ko, who confirmed that the numbers were correct, I had to get to the bottom of it. I dialed Eric up and asked, "How in the heck did you raise that much money in your first year?"

"Hmm … I don't know," he responded circumspectly. After pausing for a moment to think it through, Eric continued, "I think it's because I just really connect with Fiver from a mission standpoint. I'm always speaking passionately about the work we do when talking with friends and colleagues. When it came time to ask, I guess my friends were primed and ready to offer their support."

Eric's passion turned into wild fundraising success. Now trust me, he was no less nervous about asking his friends and colleagues for financial support than you are; this was all new to him. He didn't have the perfect pitch, and he surely couldn't predict how friends would respond to his invitation to give. But he *did* have an ace in the hole. Eric was passionate about Fiver's work, and because he regularly talked about the organization in conversations and posted about it on social media, everyone in his network already knew how deeply he was invested. When asked, his network was ready to invest too.

The most common concern we hear from board candidates as they consider joining a nonprofit board is their fear about fundraising. If you're nervous about asking people for money, you are not alone. Whether you're a first-time fundraiser or have some experience raising money for a cause, chances are the idea of asking your friends, colleagues, and family members to financially support your organization causes you a fair amount of anxiety. This chapter aims to demystify the fundraising role and introduce you to a proven approach for generating financial support from a seat on the board.

What's Your Starting Point?

To begin, take a moment to reflect on how you feel about fundraising right now.

How comfortable are you with fundraising?

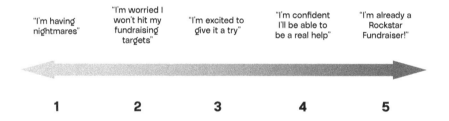

"I'm having nightmares" | "I'm worried I won't hit my fundraising targets" | "I'm excited to give it a try" | "I'm confident I'll be able to be a real help" | "I'm already a Rockstar Fundraiser!"

1   2   3   4   5

I've asked this question over and over again when training new board members. Few people place themselves on either end of the spectrum—they're not having nightmares, nor do they feel like world-class fundraisers with rock star capabilities. Most people, it turns out, are nervous about fundraising but are willing to give it a try.

I've found that the apprehension new board members experience as they step into their fundraising role revolves around a handful of common concerns:

- *They don't know where to start.* Some people believe that they have no one to ask. They don't have that fabled "Rich Uncle in Miami" in their network.

- *Fear of strained relationships.* It can be worrisome to change the dynamic of one's connection to a friend or colleague by making an "ask" for money.

- *Fear of rejection.* Some get stuck worrying about being brushed off. "What if they say no?"

- *Lack of knowledge.* New board members may feel like they're not well versed in the work of the organization and won't be able to describe it in a crisp and compelling way.

- *Lack of experience.* Most new board members have never asked a soul for money. They're nervous about falling flat on their face and straining important relationships in the process.

Don't let yourself be defeated by these familiar apprehensions. Let's get you comfortable—dare I say, excited—as you take on the fundraising role of a Causie serving on a nonprofit board.

Relax! You've Got This!

There are lots of good reasons for you to feel more comfortable with fundraising, beginning now. For starters, remember that you are not alone. Chances are that some, or even all, of your fellow board members are still learning how to fundraise, as well. Everyone starts somewhere.

Second, remember that you're not asking people to give *you* money. Instead, you're connecting your friends, colleagues, and family members with a purpose-filled opportunity to support an important cause. When you fundraise, you're asking for support on behalf of the beneficiaries of the work.

Keep in mind that fundraising as a board member is typically a team sport. You won't be thrown to the wolves and asked to raise money on your own without any support. Nonprofit organizations are fundraising enterprises. Typically, a substantial part of the revenue pie comes from philanthropic contributions, so most organizations have built a fundraising infrastructure for board members to tap into that might include an annual gala, a silent auction, a 5K charity run, an end-of-year holiday appeal, or a social media giving campaign, to name just a few.

Plus, there are likely fundraising professionals on staff to work with board members, helping you achieve your fundraising goals. You won't necessarily be the person to make the ask. Often board members serve primarily as door openers and connectors, leaving it to the CEO or the director of development to handle most of the lift in making the case, answering questions, and closing with a specific request for support.

Here's another good reason to ease your nerves about asking people to support your cause: most donors plan to make multiple charitable contributions each year. A *Donor Experience Study* by Community Brands found that nearly a third of all donors (29 percent) give to four or more causes each year, with fully half giving to two or three organizations annually.[14] While many donors have one or two organizations that receive the lion's share of their charitable giving—perhaps their house of worship, alma mater, or the organization they serve as a board member—these individuals also demonstrate a pattern of giving smaller gifts more broadly. Assume that the people in your

---

14   Paul Clolery, "People who give do it often, survey shows," The NonProfit Times, June 18, 2018, https://thenonprofittimes.com/npt_articles/people-give-often-survey-shows/.

network are planning to make several charitable gifts this year and every year thereafter. Your job as a board member is to make sure *your* organization is on the receiving end of that generosity.

Ultimately, I want to encourage you to reframe the way you think about your fundraising role. As a board member, you're inviting loved ones, friends, and colleagues to support an important cause that you are personally investing in. An ask is an invitation for those in your network to experience the same fulfillment you receive through your involvement with the organization. Think about it as an opportunity to connect them to purposefulness rather than an unwanted request.

Based on two decades of fundraising, I've learned that most people are inclined to say "Yes!" when someone they value asks for support for a cause close to their heart. So don't leave needed resources on the table. Showcase your commitment as a passionate Causie by inviting individuals in your network to invest in the organization you wholeheartedly support.

Fundraising Rules for Board Members

First and foremost, make sure you understand your organization's expectations for board member giving and fundraising. Remember that it should be a part of every board vetting process for candidates to have an open and transparent conversation with the organization's leadership about the give and give/get expectations. This aspect of board service must always be a no-surprise zone!

Second, set the pace each year by making a proud, bold, sacrificial gift. Many nonprofits ask board members to make a "personally meaningful" annual contribution to the organization they serve. "Personally meaningful" differs, of course, from individual to individual. An amount that is "personally meaningful" to a senior executive at a large publishing company, for example, is likely quite different from what would qualify as "personally meaningful" to the manager of your local independent book shop. That's as it should be. Every board member should demonstrate their passion for the mission by giving at a level that is an appropriate stretch gift for them.

I use a "feel-it-in-the-gut" test to know what the right level of giving looks like for me. As a board member, when I write a check or generate an online donation for my cause, I should feel it. I should notice it. I may even think twice about it. That, to me, is a good test to know if I'm in the right neighborhood for board giving. Now, will your contribution put you on the edge of financial ruin? No, of course not. Will you still be able to enjoy your summer family vacation? Yes. Can you still make the monthly mortgage payment? Absolutely. But you'll be proud of the gift you made, knowing that it represents an amount of money that is of real personal consequence.

Whether you write a check once a year or contribute monthly online, as a board member, lead the way. It can be unseemly to ask others to support your cause if you haven't given first. When board members give proudly and boldly at the beginning of the fiscal year, they make a statement to the organization's leadership and staff. They set a pace for their fellow board members to follow. Perhaps most importantly, they lay the groundwork to step confidently into their fundraising role.

Remember that institutional funders will take note of your giving as well, and generally expect to see 100 percent of the board making an annual donation. If the board members who serve as leaders, champions, and fiduciaries of the work aren't participating in the organization's financial success, grant officers will wonder why their foundation should be. If just one board member fails to personally contribute, it could cost the organization tens, or even hundreds, of thousands in grant dollars.

Rob's Recipe for Board Member Fundraising Success

A great deal has been written about the various stages in the fundraising process. The internet is riddled with lists and advice, and artificial intelligence (AI) chatbots can package them into whatever form you want. What I've found, however, is that those guidelines are designed for professional fundraisers working in a development department. They come off as sterile, impersonal, and transactional. In the context of a board member contemplating the most effective way to involve loved ones, close friends, and colleagues in their cause, they completely miss the mark.

Let me give you an example. Most fundraising processes describe the moment a fundraiser asks someone for support as the "solicitation" step. Solicitation is usually associated with unwanted, often persistent requests. As a paperboy during my youth, when I delivered newspapers to my neighbors, many front doors had signs prominently posted that warned, "No Solicitations!" In law school, I learned that solicitation can be associated with criminal activity. What board member is going to get excited about solicitation? I don't know about you, but I have no interest in "soliciting" my friends, colleagues, and family members for anything, much less money.

Based on two decades of real-world fundraising experience, I've found that the optimal fundraising process is much more nuanced, much more thoughtful, and much more personal than the often-cited *identification-cultivation-solicitation-stewardship* model most experts recommend.

Nuanced doesn't mean difficult, though. It simply means that there are aspects of fundraising that are vitally important but seem to get lost or overlooked, especially in the context of a board member generating financial resources through their personal network. So, with all due respect to the traditional model, I present here a new model for board member fundraising success: a recipe with seven crucial ingredients.

Rob's Recipe for Board Member Fundraising Success

1. Reflection

2. Selection

3. Connection

4. Nourishment

5. Invitation

6. Appreciation

7. Conversion

Let's break it down!

1. REFLECTION

Sit down with a pen and a pad of paper. Scroll through your mental Rolodex. Jot down the names of individuals and couples in your network, past and present, who might have an interest in your organization's work. Don't evaluate the people or their potential motivation; just write the names down that come to mind and keep moving.

Remember the number one rule of brainstorming is no judgment. Assessment will come later.

2. SELECTION

Your next step is to narrow your list to a target group of friends, colleagues, and family members who have the capacity to make a meaningful gift to your organization. Many organizations will consider a major gift to be $1,000. Others will define it as $250, $500, $2,500, or more. This determination usually depends on the size of the organization's budget and the nature of the institution's existing donor portfolio.

In addition to their capacity to give, consider the possible motivations for the people on your list. Each individual or couple you've identified as a prospective donor could be drawn to support your organization for a different reason. It's helpful to consider the range of motivations that lead people to give, and think through which one will be most compelling for each name on your list.

People typically respond positively to an invitation to give based on one or more of these eight motivations:

Common Motivations for Giving

| Mission Alignment | Faith Obligation | Enjoy a Good Party | Ego Stroke |
| Drawn to Leadership | Tax Benefits | Recognize a Loved One | Show Support |

- *Mission Alignment:* Many donors support an organization because they believe in the nonprofit's purpose and core work.

- *Faith Obligation:* Charitable giving sometimes flows from an expectation or commitment based on religious principles.

- *Enjoy a Good Party:* Some donors give to attend an organization's in-person gatherings, whether that's a lavish gala, an intimate dinner party, or something in between.

- *Ego Stroke:* Other donors seek recognition for their generosity. They're motivated by having their name listed prominently on a giving wall, engraved on a brick in the courtyard, or attached to a bench in a park.

- *Drawn to Leadership:* Donors sometimes give to demonstrate allyship with the founder, the chief executive, the gala honoree, the board chair, or another leader whom they admire.

- *Tax Benefits:* Some donors seek to take advantage of deductions or tax credits, reducing their taxable income and potentially lowering their overall tax liability.

- *Recognize a Loved One:* Some gifts are made to honor the memory or celebrate the achievements of someone special to the donor.

- *Show Support:* Many donations are made to serve as a tangible expression of solidarity and encouragement for a friend, colleague, or family member who is involved with a nonprofit organization.

You now have your target group of people who could make a meaningful gift once properly introduced to the organization. Consider listing them, including their names and likely motivation for giving. The next question is how you'll introduce them to your organization.

3. CONNECTION

As you begin to connect your prospects to the organization, prioritize making a memorable first impression. In almost every organization, there are "wow" moments that happen over the course of the year. That's the experience you want your people to have first. While a lunch meeting with the chief executive at a local restaurant might be informative, will it deeply energize your people about the work? Will it make a lasting impression about the impact the organization is having in the community? Will they enthusiastically describe their first experience with the organization over family dinner later that night?

"Wow" moments come in every shape and size, driven by the core work of the organization. Perhaps it's the "graduation" of the preschoolers as they waddle down the aisle wearing tiny robes. Maybe it's an opening night performance. The groundbreaking on the new wing of the building. The volunteer community cleanup day. The release of an animal into the wild after rehabilitation. It might be as simple as an on-site visit to observe the organization's programs in action.

Very often, board members leverage the annual gala or another fundraising event to introduce their network to the organization for the first time. I think that's suboptimal at best and often a mistake. The preferred approach for making introductions should not involve soliciting funds. Your goal is to create a meaningful connection and inspire future involvement. Putting pressure on newcomers to make a gift likely won't lead to either of those positive responses. If you get your target individuals to experience a well-designed "wow" moment, it's going to leave an indelible mark.

In addition to "wow" moments, tell your personal story about how you got involved. Share your passion for the cause. Well-meaning fundraising consultants often advise organizations to provide board members with an "elevator pitch"—a concise, carefully crafted, compelling description of the organization's work that can be delivered in the same amount of time it takes to ride an elevator. Too many board retreats dedicate hours of valuable time to co-creating this pitch, hoping to arm board members with a tool to support their fundraising and ambassadorship efforts. Using white pads and markers, they're asked to pore over every word as they create the perfect problem statement, value proposition, key differentiator, and call to action.

By and large, I've concluded that such an exercise is a waste of time. First, board members won't remember these finely tuned words when the opportunity strikes. Second, even if they were to remember the script, the rehearsed message would likely be delivered in a rote, dispassionate way. Most significantly, a one-size-fits-all elevator pitch won't capture the most powerful tool a board member has in their toolkit: a passionately conveyed, firsthand testimony recounting the profound impact they've personally witnessed the organization having in people's lives.

Fundraising is storytelling. Share your story. Provide your friends, family members, and colleagues with a memorable first impression that helps them begin to shape their own viewpoint about the organization's importance. Let them see why you're giving your valuable time, considerable talents, and hard-earned treasure to support the cause. Let your Causie passion show through.

4. NOURISHMENT

Having facilitated a memorable first impression, you've planted the seed. Now it's time to water it. Begin to nurture the relationship your friends have with the organization. Expand their connections and touchpoints with the work. Introduce them to staff members who are teeming with mission passion. Provide further exposure opportunities to the mission in action.

Nonprofit professionals often call this *friendraising,* as compared to fundraising. Friendraising is all about building meaningful connections and a sense of community to rally support for your organization. Instead of seeking financial contributions, in this stage of relationship development, your goal is to develop a network of people who genuinely care about your organization's mission. By inviting them to events, making connections to others in the organization, and providing them with informational resources, you're actively creating a supportive community that will become increasingly invested in the cause.

5. INVITATION

Once an authentic relationship is established and reinforced, it's time to invite your people to make a meaningful financial contribution in support of the cause. Here's a rule of thumb: The right person should ask for the right-sized gift to support the right initiative at the right time. Each one of those concepts matters.

> **The right person should ask for the right-sized gift to support the right initiative at the right time.**

- The *right person* to ask is the individual most likely to get a "yes" in reply. For the people in your network, that is likely you.

- The *right-sized gift* is a carefully considered, strategic amount that represents a personally meaningful contribution not outside the bounds of possibility. To ask for a gift that's too low is to leave much-needed resources on the table. To ask for a gift that's too high may demonstrate insensitivity or unpreparedness and risks souring the developing relationship with the organization.

- The *right initiative* is a stated purpose for the gift that will inspire the donor, energizing them to say "Yes!"

- The *right time*, as discussed earlier, refers to that moment when an authentic relationship has been established and the individual appears ready to deepen their involvement.

The invitation language a board member can use is actually very simple: "Charles and Sandra, will you consider a leadership gift in the amount of $5,000 to support this vital new initiative?" Then, stop talking. Give them the space to respond. If need be, sit uncomfortably in silence. Don't back away from the invitation, discount it, or apologize.

If this invitation moment sounds terrifying, perhaps you're not the right person to deliver it, at least not until you become more comfortable in the board fundraising role. Instead, offer to serve on an *asking team* that includes you as the relationship owner, as well as either the chief executive or a development team member. I've occasionally participated as a member of an *asking team* in which my primary role was to arrange a lunch meeting, invite the participants, and pay the check. When it came time to describe the need and make the ask, the organization's staff team was better positioned to make the case than me.

6. APPRECIATION

As soon as a gift is made, express your gratitude. The individuals in your network who donate will want to experience your heartfelt appreciation right away. It will be gratifying for them to hear how much their commitment to support your cause means to you.

In years gone by, this typically meant a personal handwritten note, a formal acknowledgment letter, and a gracious telephone call.

Increasingly, this is becoming a lost art. Today, an expression of appreciation might more likely take the form of a text or voice message sent to the donor's cell phone. But do you want to really blow your donor friend away? Pen a heartfelt note and send it via snail mail. It may be the only handwritten piece of mail they receive all month or even all year.

Personally thanking those donors you connected to the organization is important, but so is thanking donors you don't yet know. Supporters feel appreciated when they hear from a board member who "just wants to say thank you." In fact, an immediate expression of thanks is not just gracious, it's strategic. A study by Penelope Burk, author of *Donor-Centered Fundraising*, found that supporters who were thanked within forty-eight hours of making their first gift gave 39 percent more with their next contribution as compared with those who did not receive a timely expression of appreciation.[15] Listen to fundraising expert Claire Axelrad who calls a simple follow-up thank-you call "your secret weapon."[16]

7. CONVERSION

The final ingredient in my recipe is to convert your donor friend into a true believer. Find a way to get them on the inside team. Engaged donors are repeat donors.

When I was at CGLA, we received a $1,000 check from a donor I'd never heard of before. I called to become acquainted and soon after had a lunch date arranged with Cate Northup. Over a sandwich and soup, I learned that Cate was a stay-at-home mom, focused on raising her kids after a rewarding career in advertising, branding, and

---

15   Penelope Burk, Donor-Centered Fundraising (Herndon, VA: Burk & Associates, Ltd., 2003).

16   Claire Axelrad, "Six keys to rock thank you calls and retain more donors," clarification.com, April 26, 2016, https://clairification.com/2016/04/26/6-keys-rock-thank-calls-retain-donors/.

marketing. After paying the bill, I asked Cate if she would consider helping build CGLA's marketing platform, describing the many weaknesses I saw in its present state.

Before long, Cate was coming into the office once a week as a pro bono consultant, managing our website, building content, and growing the organization's social media profile. We even assigned Cate a cubicle, helping her feel more connected as a member of the team. When the next annual gala rolled around, I asked Cate and her husband Cary to serve as co-chairs of the planning committee. Not only did they provide inspired leadership to the event, but they also made a contribution significantly larger than their first donation. By bringing Cate into the organization as an insider, she'd fallen in love with the work. She was all in. Cate had found her cause.

What does it look like to convert your donor friend into a true believer and get them on the inside team? Brainstorm ideas with your organization's leadership. Be creative; the opportunities are endless. By bringing them into the organization's community in a meaningful and more formally connected way, you'll create a repeat donor who will almost certainly grow their financial commitment as they simultaneously dedicate their time and talent to the work.

A Final Word

The fundraising team at your organization works hard, year-round, to drive revenue into the organization. At the beginning of every fiscal year, their core metric clicks back to zero as they begin yet another climb up the revenue mountain to achieve ambitious targets. They ask and ask for support, receiving plenty of rejection in return. They meticulously plan events, spearhead campaigns, and sit for countless meals with donors. They write innumerable grant proposals, as well, the vast majority of which will receive a curt response that includes the word, "Unfortunately …" Their role can be somewhat lonely, as well, sitting adjacent to the program team doing the front-line work of the organization. In short, being a full-time fundraiser is a tough job.

As a board member, make it your mission to let them know how much you appreciate what they do. A simple "thank you" for their hard work can go a long way. Give them a moment of public recognition at the board meeting. Take them to their favorite restaurant for a special "I appreciate you" lunch—on you, of course.

Oh, and one more thing. Want to know how to really make the development team feel the love? I'll say it one more time. Make your personally meaningful, bold, proud, annual contribution on the first day of the fiscal year. Don't wait until they ask you for it. Don't make them track you down. I've had board members drop by my office and hand me a nice-sized check in person. A simple gesture like this will speak volumes about your solidarity with the team. It is the clearest way to demonstrate your genuine appreciation for their work and your commitment to supporting their efforts in securing the funds vital for mission success.

Reflection Questions

1. Revisit our poll from the beginning of this chapter. Have you moved to the right on the continuum? What has contributed to your increased confidence as you step into the board fundraising role?

How comfortable are you with fundraising?

"I'm having nightmares"	"I'm worried I won't hit my fundraising targets"	"I'm excited to give it a try"	"I'm confident I'll be able to be a real help"	"I'm already a Rockstar Fundraiser!"
1	2	3	4	5

2. Use the feel-it-in-the-gut test to consider what a proud, bold, sacrificial, personal gift will look like for you. How much will you be prepared to contribute in your first year as a board member?

3. Reflection is the first step in *Rob's Recipe for Board Member Fundraising Success*. Take a few minutes to begin the process right now. Scroll through your mental Rolodex, jotting down the names of individuals and couples in your network, past and present, who might have an interest in your organization's work.

4. Fundraising is storytelling. What story will you tell about your organization? Make sure to let your Causie passion show through.

Chapter
Nine

Elevating and Transforming Governance in the Nonprofit Sector

The purpose of life is to live a life of purpose.

—RICHARD LEIDER, *THE POWER OF PURPOSE*

Remember that conversation I mentioned during lunch with a nonprofit CEO, back when I decided to leave my job and embark on the journey of founding Cause Strategy Partners? I wrote about it in chapter 5. The poignant advice was this: "Rob, do the sector a favor. If you're going to put your time and energy into this, do something different. Be disruptive. Nonprofits don't need any more mediocre board members."

Well, I took those words to heart. We are indeed bringing about meaningful change, but not in a reckless "move-fast-and-break-things" manner; frankly, that's just not my style. I prefer a more deliberate approach—rooted in research, driven by organic growth, and inspired by passion.

Cause Strategy Partners was born out of a deep desire to revolutionize governance in the nonprofit sector. I wanted to identify what led to subpar boards and then tackle those issues head-on, systematically, and with purpose. As thousands, and eventually tens of thousands, of board members embrace the approach to board service outlined in this book, the landscape of nonprofit governance will undergo a transformation.

You see, the present state of nonprofit governance is not okay. Too many boards are disengaged. Too many board members position their board service low on their list of personal priorities. Too many board meetings are poorly attended, regularly struggling to achieve quorum or keep directors in their seats to the end of the meeting. Too many nonprofit chief executives feel unsupported by those who should be their partners in leadership.

It's easy to conclude that such mediocre engagement stems from apathy. You might think, "These individuals aren't committed to advancing the organization's mission. They simply don't care." And you could be onto something; indeed, some boards consist of individuals whose personal passions haven't aligned with the organization's mission from the beginning. Essentially, they're the wrong fit for the role.

Therein lies the first factor contributing to mediocre nonprofit board governance: the people in the boardroom. Either the cause of the organization isn't *their* cause, or they haven't been adequately trained on their roles and responsibilities. And therein lies the second factor. As Archilocus explained, "We don't rise to the level of our expectations, we fall to the level of our training." When faced with high-pressure situations, our performance isn't determined by what we hope or expect to achieve but rather by the level of preparation and training we have undergone.

But there's more going on. Typically, the individuals who end up in the boardroom were selected through a traditional and ineffective board development approach—having been tapped on the shoulder by an existing board member to fill a vacant position. What often results is a homogeneous board that doesn't reflect the community served and lacks a deep dedication to the mission. An "OK-I-guess-if-you-need-me" board member won't likely become a Causie.

On the flip side, it's not entirely fair to put all the blame on the board member doing the shoulder-tapping, especially when the candidate being approached says yes. Many people end up in a governing role because serving on a board is an honor or they wanted to support a friend. They hadn't taken the time to explore their *own* sense of purpose and identify *their* cause.

In so many ways, board development hasn't traditionally been approached in a passion-forward way. What we truly need is a governance transformation—a shift in the very definition of what it means to be a nonprofit board member. That's what I've tried to lay out in this book: a Causie Movement that can transform governance in the nonprofit sector.

A Causie Movement

I think everyone is a potential Causie. Deep down, everyone has a cause to care passionately about, even if they haven't fully recognized or uncovered it yet. Imagine if the majority of people in your community, workplace, or social circle took the time to work through chapter 2 of this book, "Finding Your Cause." It's likely that their head and their heart would guide them toward at least one area of societal need that's closely aligned with their personal values and interests. Causies have agency; the trajectory of their community service is in *their* hands. They're not waiting for someone to find them. If this became a widespread practice, the nonprofit sector would undergo a remarkable metamorphosis. Dare I say that society itself would be profoundly transformed.

Causies endeavor to find the best possible organization that aligns with the change they want to make in the world. Their personal mission extends well beyond simply securing a board seat—it's about moving the dial on an important cause. The end point for most Causies is that one cause is never enough.

I founded Cause Strategy Partners to help busy people like you find their purpose and drive meaningful societal change. You've likely heard the phrase, "Start with why." Author Simon Sinek wrote a terrific book with that very title. That is the right starting point to be sure, but I have also found that both an organization and an individual will likely see their "why" evolve over time. That certainly happened in my life and with my firm. The first "why" of Cause Strategy Partners was very clear, flowing from my New Year's resolution—the story I shared at the beginning of this book. From there, our core purpose has expanded to include six "whys"—six core reasons we do the work we do. These six statements describe the essence of the Causie Movement.

TO CHALLENGE APATHY AND DISENGAGEMENT

Of the countless board members I'd served alongside over the years, some were stellar, others were largely absent or disengaged, and a handful could even be described as harmful to the mission. But the majority would best be described as so-so contributors.

Equally frustrating, I was finding that most professionals I would meet in social or business settings were not serving any cause, in any capacity. Despite their exceptional professional experience, wisdom learned from life, well-honed skills, ability to make financial contributions, and robust network to draw on for support, so many of these professionals had simply not made service a part of their personal or professional journey.

My primary goal was rather straightforward in 2015: connect talented professionals to their cause, provide them with effective governance training, and once serving on a board, provide ongoing evaluation and support so they're both equipped and accountable to do the job right. I was convinced we could ask more of nonprofit board members because they wanted to give more of themselves. Since 2015, the Causies we affectionately refer to as BoardLeaders have been proving that my assumption was right.

TO MAKE BOARD DEVELOPMENT MORE STRATEGIC

The second "why" behind our work was to make board development more strategic. Imagine a talented mid-career professional who stands ready, willing, and able to serve their cause as a board member. Without BoardLead or another board matching program, how is that professional likely to find a board seat? The answer, I was finding, was this: wait to be tapped on the shoulder by a friend asking, "Would you be interested in joining my board?" That's not strategic board development; that's happenstance.

By breaking down the wall that stands between candidates and social good organizations, BoardLead nonprofit partners meet values-aligned professionals from terrific companies with great skills who begin their board journey committed to full board engagement and trained in governance. The purpose of this book is to build on this "why," taking everything we've learned about effective board matching, training, and support and making it available to *anyone* who is ready to become a Causie.

TO SHIFT POWER DYNAMICS IN THE
DIRECTION OF NONPROFITS

Third, I wanted to empower nonprofits to select candidates for the board who were ready to go all in. In traditional board development, a governance committee solicits potential board member names, decides on who to approach, and then begins the process of assessing the interests of those on the shortlist. The organization chooses and then woos the candidate.

Through our work at Cause Strategy Partners, board candidates select their top-choice nonprofits among a competitive field of other exceptional candidates. We make the match and introduction, offer training, and then set our candidates loose to make the case to the organization's leadership, articulating how they'll advance the mission. The candidate chooses and then woos the organization.

That simple shift in the power dynamics of the board development process is game-changing and has turned BoardLead into a trusted partner as nonprofit organizations come back to us year after year to meet more candidates who are interested in their cause. Mission passion is the central driver of our work.

TO MAKE BOARD SERVICE MORE ACCESSIBLE TO
HISTORICALLY UNDERREPRESENTED GROUPS

Not many years ago, nonprofit board service was largely reserved for society's well-heeled, well-placed elite. In some instances, we still see that misguided board development strategy today. It's outdated, it's ineffective, and it can also be dangerous.

In the corporate realm, nonprofit board service opportunities have traditionally been reserved for the C-suite. It's no secret, of course, that the C-suite has historically been occupied by leaders who are more senior, more likely to be white, and more likely to be male than the company's rank and file.

Through the work of Cause Strategy Partners, our corporate partners are now able to reach much further into the organizational chart and get their people elected to community leadership positions at scale. We break down walls that separate talented professionals from serving their cause. We've also been able to address one of the most pervasive governance challenges across the country: building nonprofit boards that are racially and ethnically diverse. I'm so proud that through focused, organization-wide effort, 56 percent of our elected BoardLeaders identify as people of color, which is approaching triple the national average of 22 percent.[17]

TO BE A LEADER IN THE MOVEMENT TO MAKE BUSINESS A FORCE FOR GOOD

A fifth motivation driving our work is to model what responsible business looks like. Our B-Corps Certification speaks to the purposeful structure of our organization and the social impact outcomes we are achieving. We have been named a global Top Impact Company by Real Leaders four years in a row and counting. Over our first nine years, Cause Strategy Partners donated more than $330,000 to community causes, representing 2 percent of our total revenue and a much greater percentage of our profits. Our team members serve on governing and ancillary boards representing an array of cause areas. Remarkably, our BoardLeaders generate more than $24 million each year in giving and fundraising dollars for the organizations they serve, our nonprofit partners. The concept of "purpose over profit" is an important value that will always guide our work.

---

17   BoardSource, "Leading with intent: BoardSource index of nonprofit board practices," 2021, https://delawarenonprofit.org/wp-content/uploads/2022/09/2021-Leading-with-Intent-Report.pdf.

TO ELEVATE AND TRANSFORM GOVERNANCE
IN THE SOCIAL GOOD SECTOR

Nearly a decade into the journey, today we seek to do much more than challenge apathy and disengagement. The Causie Movement aspires to set a new standard of what nonprofit board service must look like. There must be no room for disengagement, absence, or mediocrity in leading social good organizations. We believe there should be no difference between how leaders serve corporate boards and how they serve nonprofit boards. Both require a strong sense of duty, focused attention, and a determined commitment to the organization's mission. Our communities, our kids, our seniors, our impoverished, our sick, our students, our displaced, our environment—they all deserve the very best of what each one of us can bring to our cause.

Reflection Questions

- How will you help elevate governance at the nonprofit you serve?

- What unhelpful or harmful behaviors have you noticed among your fellow board members?

- Specifically, what can you do to model behaviors or actions that set a new standard of excellence for your colleagues on the board?

Conclusion

The end is where we start from.
—T. S. ELIOT, "LITTLE GIDDING"
(FROM *FOUR QUARTETS*)

As I reflect on the journey we've taken together, I am full of hope. Through my work, I've witnessed the dramatic impact just one busy individual can have in the world when they identify and then begin to support and serve their cause. I've watched thousands of business professionals take leadership roles on nonprofit boards, enriching their own lives while simultaneously sparking meaningful and lasting change at the organizations they serve and support.

I'm continually inspired by those who have embraced the call to fully engaged board service, bringing their skills, talents, and passions to organizations pursuing vital missions. These individuals have become Causies, reordering important aspects of their lives—the way they invest their time, the dedicated use of their skills, the people they spend time with after work, and their household budget, for example—to make an intentional, substantial, long-term commitment to serve their cause. They serve as a testament to the transformative power of purpose-driven board leadership, and they're an inspiration.

Through the pages of this book, I've shared insights and strategies aimed at elevating the core expectations of governance within the nonprofit sector. It is my sincere hope that these principles will guide your Causie journey. My earnest wish is that the lessons of this book will serve as a catalyst for transformation in the social good sector, sparking a renewed commitment to excellence and integrity among nonprofit board members across the globe.

As we look ahead, I pose a question to you, the reader who has invested time on this journey with me: *What will be your cause? What mark will you leave on the world?* Becoming a Causie isn't merely about serving on a board; it's about embracing a lifelong journey of impact and service.

I challenge you to embark on the journey outlined in this book—from finding your cause to leading a nonprofit from a board seat as one who is consumed with mission impact. And after you've completed one such journey, I urge you to do it again and again. Let your life's work be a testament to the power of purpose-driven leadership, a legacy of meaningful impact and service.

I invite you to join us in building a Causie Movement: a global community of like-minded individuals committed to driving positive change in the world. Share this book with a friend; tell the HR, talent development, or community affairs team at your company about BoardLead; or advocate for the importance of fully engaged board service at the nonprofit you're serving. Together, we can create a network of changemakers, united by a common purpose and a shared commitment to elevating and transforming governance in the nonprofit sector.

I also want to invite you to stay connected by joining our Causie Community, a platform for inspiration, idea-sharing, and collaboration. Together, let's continue to inspire, empower, and support one another as we make serving our cause an important aspect of our personal and professional identity. To sign up, visit www.robacton.com.

Let's end where we began, with the powerful question penned by Steven Schwartz in *Pippin*—"Don't you see I want my life to be something more than long?" It's time to answer that question. I urge you to become a Causie, support and serve your cause, embrace the power of fully engaged board leadership, and leave an indelible mark on the world.

Epilogue

The Invisible Red Thread

"You know you're a red thread, right?"

"I'm sorry, Johnathan?"

Reframing the question, more slowly: "You're a red thread. Did you know that?"

Johnathan Lay, a poet friend I'd met a few years earlier at a coffee shop in San Francisco, looked me straight in the eye over dinner, awaiting my response. Not having any idea what he was talking about, I asked for more.

"A red thread is hard to define." He went on to explain that the concept stems from both Eastern and Western cultures and is rooted in various mythologies.

Now I was leaning into the conversation. "So what exactly is a red thread?"

The origin of the concept, he continued, is an ancient Chinese myth of two lovers connected by an invisible red thread, destined to be together.

As I started to roll my eyes, Johnathan cut me off.

"But that notion is too romantic, in my opinion," he continued. "A red thread is someone connected to other people, all of whom were destined to meet in order to strengthen one another's lives and do good in the world."

Those words caught my attention. I've always said the best thing I have to offer the world is the incredible relationships I've developed over the years. I've often felt like it was wild luck to meet and build connections with so many strangers who would go on to change my life for the better. And now, through my work over the last decade, I've been fortunate to play a role in connecting thousands of exceptionally talented people to others with similar values to their own, committed to serving a cause at the center of their collective passion.

Now, believe me, I understand the instinct to shake one's head and dismiss the concept outright. Words like "mythical" and "destined to meet" cause me to react with a silent scoff. After all, I'm a lawyer trained to use evidence to build a case. I get the pessimism.

A red thread network? A secret society? A group destined to be connected? At the time, I shrugged off the conversation as an inventive concept conjured up by my well-read, artistic, and imaginative poet friend. But the concept never left me.

This idea that a group of people are unknowingly joined together, destined to one day meet, has become quite compelling for me. In many ways, the parable captures my life's journey and—even more specifically—my experience serving on nonprofit boards. By joining forces with Causies who share my values, my passions, and my viewpoint on what a better world would look like, teamed with a determination to do something about it, I *have* become a better person, and I *have* been able to make a difference on causes that are close to my heart.

Without them—without the invisible red thread bringing us together, if you will—my life's journey would have been far less fulfilling, meaningful, and impactful. That, I can assure you, isn't mystical at all. It is fundamentally, verifiably true.

Rob
Acton

About the Author

Rob Acton is the founder and CEO of Cause Strategy Partners, a social impact consulting firm that connects executives and employees of Fortune 500 companies and global professional services firms in the United States and United Kingdom with opportunities to serve on nonprofit boards. Through the firm's proprietary technology, innovative process, and team of experts, BoardLead—an award-winning nonprofit board placement, training, and support program—has helped thousands of professionals find their cause. The firm's offerings include BoardLearn, an online governance training platform, as well as an Executive Concierge Board Placement service focused on connecting C-suite leaders to high-impact board leadership opportunities. Cause Strategy Partners' client list includes scores of preeminent companies across a wide range of industries.

Rob has nearly three decades of experience founding, leading, and scaling social good organizations as both a chief executive and board leader. He served for eleven years as executive director of two nonprofit organizations: Taproot Foundation in New York City and Cabrini Green Legal Aid in Chicago.

A recognized expert on nonprofit governance and leadership, Rob has trained thousands of professionals on high-impact board service.

He has served on numerous governing boards, advisory boards, and state commissions. Rob currently chairs the board of directors of Broadway Inspirational Voices in New York City, where he resides.

Rob's causes are second chances for formerly incarcerated individuals, nonprofit capacity building, and the performing arts.

Appendix

Process Matters: Board Member Development

Preparation

1 Identify Needs

Assess current composition and prioritize gap areas

- Keep a Board Matrix highlighting gaps across the full range of diversity needs
- Set recruitment priorities
- Identify a board development champion; not the chief executive

2 Identify Candidates

Develop a pool of talented, diverse candidates

- Focus on the recruitment priorities
- Cast a wide net
- Source through multiple channels
- Be ambitious – aim for superstars

Exploration

3 First Meeting

Provide key information and assess alignment

- Meet in person with board candidates
- Choose your staff representative wisely
- Be prepared: know the candidate's background and articulate how they can uniquely drive impact
- Clearly communicate next steps

4 Onsite Visit

Give your candidate a memorable experience

- Invite candidate to see the programs and services in action
- Have onsite visit led by senior staff member and/or Board member
- Help candidate experience the mission, values and culture in person
- Allow time and space for questions

Vetting

5 Additional Touch Points

Win board buy-in and answer candidate questions

- Have at least three board members meet with the candidate
- Provide candidate with additional perspectives: client, senior staff, etc.
- Discuss board expectations directly: giving, fundraising, the "give/get," time commitment, committee service

6 Agree on Nomination

Make an informed decision and communicate clearly

- Ensure all board member questions and concerns are addressed before inviting candidate to join the board
- If the board decides not to move forward, call the candidate, sharing candidly why the fit is not right at this time

Engagement

7 Election

Add candidate to the slate of nominated board members

- Invite candidate to attend the Board meeting in which they will be elected
- Elect slate at top of agenda; give the opportunity for your new board member to jump right in
- Set high expectations for new board members; ask them to stretch themselves

8 Onboarding

Give your new board member resources to start strong

- Provide your new board member with a board handbook containing a wealth of key resources
- Offer a New Board Member Orientation program for newly elected Directors
- Consider assigning a board mentor to help acclimate and answer questions

Cause Strategy Partners

Form **990**

Return of Organization Exempt From Income Tax

Under section 501(c), 527, or 4947(a)(1) of the Internal Revenue Code (except private foundations)

Do not enter social security numbers on this form as it may be made public.

Go to *www.irs.gov/Form990* for instructions and the latest information.

OMB No. 1545-0047

2023

Open to Public Inspection

Department of the Treasury
Internal Revenue Service

A For the 2023 calendar year, or tax year beginning _____ , 2023, and ending _____ , 20 _____

B Check if applicable:	**C** Name of organization				**D** Employer identification number
☐ Address change	Doing business as				
☐ Name change	Number and street (or P.O. box if mail is not delivered to street address)		Room/suite		**E** Telephone number
☐ Initial return					
☐ Final return/terminated	City or town, state or province, country, and ZIP or foreign postal code				
☐ Amended return					**G** Gross receipts $
☐ Application pending	**F** Name and address of principal officer:				

H(a) Is this a group return for subordinates? ☐ Yes ☐ No
H(b) Are all subordinates included? ☐ Yes ☐ No
If "No," attach a list. See instructions.

I Tax-exempt status: ☐ 501(c)(3) ☐ 501(c) ( ) (insert no.) ☐ 4947(a)(1) or ☐ 527

J Website:

H(c) Group exemption number

K Form of organization: ☐ Corporation ☐ Trust ☐ Association ☐ Other _____ **L** Year of formation: _____ **M** State of legal domicile: _____

Part I Summary

Activities & Governance

1 Briefly describe the organization's mission or most significant activities: _____

2 Check this box ☐ if the organization discontinued its operations or disposed of more than 25% of its net assets.

3	Number of voting members of the governing body (Part VI, line 1a)	**3**
4	Number of independent voting members of the governing body (Part VI, line 1b)	**4**
5	Total number of individuals employed in calendar year 2023 (Part V, line 2a)	**5**
6	Total number of volunteers (estimate if necessary)	**6**
7a	Total unrelated business revenue from Part VIII, column (C), line 12	**7a**
b	Net unrelated business taxable income from Form 990-T, Part I, line 11	**7b**

Revenue

		Prior Year	Current Year
8	Contributions and grants (Part VIII, line 1h)		
9	Program service revenue (Part VIII, line 2g)		
10	Investment income (Part VIII, column (A), lines 3, 4, and 7d)		
11	Other revenue (Part VIII, column (A), lines 5, 6d, 8c, 9c, 10c, and 11e) . . .		
12	Total revenue—add lines 8 through 11 (must equal Part VIII, column (A), line 12)		

Expenses

13	Grants and similar amounts paid (Part IX, column (A), lines 1–3)		
14	Benefits paid to or for members (Part IX, column (A), line 4)		
15	Salaries, other compensation, employee benefits (Part IX, column (A), lines 5–10)		
16a	Professional fundraising fees (Part IX, column (A), line 11e)		
b	Total fundraising expenses (Part IX, column (D), line 25) _____		
17	Other expenses (Part IX, column (A), lines 11a–11d, 11f–24e)		
18	Total expenses. Add lines 13–17 (must equal Part IX, column (A), line 25) .		
19	Revenue less expenses. Subtract line 18 from line 12		

Net Assets or Fund Balances

		Beginning of Current Year	End of Year
20	Total assets (Part X, line 16)		
21	Total liabilities (Part X, line 26)		
22	Net assets or fund balances. Subtract line 21 from line 20		

Part II Signature Block

Under penalties of perjury, I declare that I have examined this return, including accompanying schedules and statements, and to the best of my knowledge and belief, it is true, correct, and complete. Declaration of preparer (other than officer) is based on all information of which preparer has any knowledge.

Sign Here

Signature of officer	Date
Type or print name and title	

Paid Preparer Use Only

Print/Type preparer's name	Preparer's signature	Date	Check ☐ if self-employed	PTIN
Firm's name			Firm's EIN	
Firm's address			Phone no.	

May the IRS discuss this return with the preparer shown above? See instructions . . . . ☐ Yes ☐ No

For Paperwork Reduction Act Notice, see the separate instructions. Cat. No. 11282Y Form **990** (2023)

Part III   **Statement of Program Service Accomplishments**
Check if Schedule O contains a response or note to any line in this Part III . . . . ☐

1   Briefly describe the organization's mission:

----

2   Did the organization undertake any significant program services during the year which were not listed on the prior Form 990 or 990-EZ? . . . . ☐ **Yes** ☐ **No**
If "Yes," describe these new services on Schedule O.

3   Did the organization cease conducting, or make significant changes in how it conducts, any program services? . . . . ☐ **Yes** ☐ **No**
If "Yes," describe these changes on Schedule O.

4   Describe the organization's program service accomplishments for each of its three largest program services, as measured by expenses. Section 501(c)(3) and 501(c)(4) organizations are required to report the amount of grants and allocations to others, the total expenses, and revenue, if any, for each program service reported.

4a   (Code: _____) (Expenses $ _____ including grants of $ _____) (Revenue $ _____)

4b   (Code: _____) (Expenses $ _____ including grants of $ _____) (Revenue $ _____)

4c   (Code: _____) (Expenses $ _____ including grants of $ _____) (Revenue $ _____)

4d   Other program services (Describe on Schedule O.)
(Expenses $ _____ including grants of $ _____) (Revenue $ _____)

4e   Total program service expenses ►

Form **990** (2023)

Form 990 (2023)   Page **3**

Part IV   Checklist of Required Schedules

			Yes	No
1	Is the organization described in section 501(c)(3) or 4947(a)(1) (other than a private foundation)? *If "Yes," complete Schedule A*	**1**		
2	Is the organization required to complete Schedule B, Schedule of Contributors? See instructions	**2**		
3	Did the organization engage in direct or indirect political campaign activities on behalf of or in opposition to candidates for public office? *If "Yes," complete Schedule C, Part I*	**3**		
4	**Section 501(c)(3) organizations.** Did the organization engage in lobbying activities, or have a section 501(h) election in effect during the tax year? *If "Yes," complete Schedule C, Part II*	**4**		
5	Is the organization a section 501(c)(4), 501(c)(5), or 501(c)(6) organization that receives membership dues, assessments, or similar amounts as defined in Rev. Proc. 98-19? *If "Yes," complete Schedule C, Part III* .	**5**		
6	Did the organization maintain any donor advised funds or any similar funds or accounts for which donors have the right to provide advice on the distribution or investment of amounts in such funds or accounts? *If "Yes," complete Schedule D, Part I*	**6**		
7	Did the organization receive or hold a conservation easement, including easements to preserve open space, the environment, historic land areas, or historic structures? *If "Yes," complete Schedule D, Part II* . . .	**7**		
8	Did the organization maintain collections of works of art, historical treasures, or other similar assets? *If "Yes," complete Schedule D, Part III*	**8**		
9	Did the organization report an amount in Part X, line 21, for escrow or custodial account liability; serve as a custodian for amounts not listed in Part X; or provide credit counseling, debt management, credit repair, or debt negotiation services? *If "Yes," complete Schedule D, Part IV*	**9**		
10	Did the organization, directly or through a related organization, hold assets in donor-restricted endowments or in quasi-endowments? *If "Yes," complete Schedule D, Part V*	**10**		
11	If the organization's answer to any of the following questions is "Yes," then complete Schedule D, Parts VI, VII, VIII, IX, or X, as applicable.			
a	Did the organization report an amount for land, buildings, and equipment in Part X, line 10? *If "Yes," complete Schedule D, Part VI*	**11a**		
b	Did the organization report an amount for investments—other securities in Part X, line 12, that is 5% or more of its total assets reported in Part X, line 16? *If "Yes," complete Schedule D, Part VII*	**11b**		
c	Did the organization report an amount for investments—program related in Part X, line 13, that is 5% or more of its total assets reported in Part X, line 16? *If "Yes," complete Schedule D, Part VIII*	**11c**		
d	Did the organization report an amount for other assets in Part X, line 15, that is 5% or more of its total assets reported in Part X, line 16? *If "Yes," complete Schedule D, Part IX*	**11d**		
e	Did the organization report an amount for other liabilities in Part X, line 25? *If "Yes," complete Schedule D, Part X*	**11e**		
f	Did the organization's separate or consolidated financial statements for the tax year include a footnote that addresses the organization's liability for uncertain tax positions under FIN 48 (ASC 740)? *If "Yes," complete Schedule D, Part X*	**11f**		
12a	Did the organization obtain separate, independent audited financial statements for the tax year? *If "Yes," complete Schedule D, Parts XI and XII*	**12a**		
b	Was the organization included in consolidated, independent audited financial statements for the tax year? *If "Yes," and if the organization answered "No" to line 12a, then completing Schedule D, Parts XI and XII is optional*	**12b**		
13	Is the organization a school described in section 170(b)(1)(A)(ii)? *If "Yes," complete Schedule E* . . .	**13**		
14a	Did the organization maintain an office, employees, or agents outside of the United States?	**14a**		
b	Did the organization have aggregate revenues or expenses of more than $10,000 from grantmaking, fundraising, business, investment, and program service activities outside the United States, or aggregate foreign investments valued at $100,000 or more? *If "Yes," complete Schedule F, Parts I and IV*.	**14b**		
15	Did the organization report on Part IX, column (A), line 3, more than $5,000 of grants or other assistance to or for any foreign organization? *If "Yes," complete Schedule F, Parts II and IV*	**15**		
16	Did the organization report on Part IX, column (A), line 3, more than $5,000 of aggregate grants or other assistance to or for foreign individuals? *If "Yes," complete Schedule F, Parts III and IV*.	**16**		
17	Did the organization report a total of more than $15,000 of expenses for professional fundraising services on Part IX, column (A), lines 6 and 11e? *If "Yes," complete Schedule G, Part I. See instructions*	**17**		
18	Did the organization report more than $15,000 total of fundraising event gross income and contributions on Part VIII, lines 1c and 8a? *If "Yes," complete Schedule G, Part II*	**18**		
19	Did the organization report more than $15,000 of gross income from gaming activities on Part VIII, line 9a? *If "Yes," complete Schedule G, Part III*	**19**		
20a	Did the organization operate one or more hospital facilities? *If "Yes," complete Schedule H*	**20a**		
b	If "Yes" to line 20a, did the organization attach a copy of its audited financial statements to this return? .	**20b**		
21	Did the organization report more than $5,000 of grants or other assistance to any domestic organization or domestic government on Part IX, column (A), line 1? *If "Yes," complete Schedule I, Parts I and II*	**21**		

Form **990** (2023)

Part IV Checklist of Required Schedules *(continued)*

			Yes	No
22	Did the organization report more than $5,000 of grants or other assistance to or for domestic individuals on Part IX, column (A), line 2? *If "Yes," complete Schedule I, Parts I and III*	**22**		
23	Did the organization answer "Yes" to Part VII, Section A, line 3, 4, or 5, about compensation of the organization's current and former officers, directors, trustees, key employees, and highest compensated employees? *If "Yes," complete Schedule J*	**23**		
24a	Did the organization have a tax-exempt bond issue with an outstanding principal amount of more than $100,000 as of the last day of the year, that was issued after December 31, 2002? *If "Yes," answer lines 24b through 24d and complete Schedule K. If "No," go to line 25a*	**24a**		
b	Did the organization invest any proceeds of tax-exempt bonds beyond a temporary period exception? . .	**24b**		
c	Did the organization maintain an escrow account other than a refunding escrow at any time during the year to defease any tax-exempt bonds?	**24c**		
d	Did the organization act as an "on behalf of" issuer for bonds outstanding at any time during the year? . .	**24d**		
25a	**Section 501(c)(3), 501(c)(4), and 501(c)(29) organizations.** Did the organization engage in an excess benefit transaction with a disqualified person during the year? *If "Yes," complete Schedule L, Part I*	**25a**		
b	Is the organization aware that it engaged in an excess benefit transaction with a disqualified person in a prior year, and that the transaction has not been reported on any of the organization's prior Forms 990 or 990-EZ? *If "Yes," complete Schedule L, Part I*	**25b**		
26	Did the organization report any amount on Part X, line 5 or 22, for receivables from or payables to any current or former officer, director, trustee, key employee, creator or founder, substantial contributor, or 35% controlled entity or family member of any of these persons? *If "Yes," complete Schedule L, Part II* . . .	**26**		
27	Did the organization provide a grant or other assistance to any current or former officer, director, trustee, key employee, creator or founder, substantial contributor or employee thereof, a grant selection committee member, or to a 35% controlled entity (including an employee thereof) or family member of any of these persons? *If "Yes," complete Schedule L, Part III*	**27**		
28	Was the organization a party to a business transaction with one of the following parties? (See the Schedule L, Part IV, instructions for applicable filing thresholds, conditions, and exceptions).			
a	A current or former officer, director, trustee, key employee, creator or founder, or substantial contributor? *If "Yes," complete Schedule L, Part IV*	**28a**		
b	A family member of any individual described in line 28a? *If "Yes," complete Schedule L, Part IV*	**28b**		
c	A 35% controlled entity of one or more individuals and/or organizations described in line 28a or 28b? *If "Yes," complete Schedule L, Part IV*	**28c**		
29	Did the organization receive more than $25,000 in noncash contributions? *If "Yes," complete Schedule M*	**29**		
30	Did the organization receive contributions of art, historical treasures, or other similar assets, or qualified conservation contributions? *If "Yes," complete Schedule M*	**30**		
31	Did the organization liquidate, terminate, or dissolve and cease operations? *If "Yes," complete Schedule N, Part I*	**31**		
32	Did the organization sell, exchange, dispose of, or transfer more than 25% of its net assets? *If "Yes," complete Schedule N, Part II*	**32**		
33	Did the organization own 100% of an entity disregarded as separate from the organization under Regulations sections 301.7701-2 and 301.7701-3? *If "Yes," complete Schedule R, Part I*	**33**		
34	Was the organization related to any tax-exempt or taxable entity? *If "Yes," complete Schedule R, Part II, III, or IV, and Part V, line 1*	**34**		
35a	Did the organization have a controlled entity within the meaning of section 512(b)(13)?	**35a**		
b	If "Yes" to line 35a, did the organization receive any payment from or engage in any transaction with a controlled entity within the meaning of section 512(b)(13)? *If "Yes," complete Schedule R, Part V, line 2* . .	**35b**		
36	**Section 501(c)(3) organizations.** Did the organization make any transfers to an exempt non-charitable related organization? *If "Yes," complete Schedule R, Part V, line 2*	**36**		
37	Did the organization conduct more than 5% of its activities through an entity that is not a related organization and that is treated as a partnership for federal income tax purposes? *If "Yes," complete Schedule R, Part VI*	**37**		
38	Did the organization complete Schedule O and provide explanations on Schedule O for Part VI, lines 11b and 19? **Note:** All Form 990 filers are required to complete Schedule O	**38**		

Part V Statements Regarding Other IRS Filings and Tax Compliance

Check if Schedule O contains a response or note to any line in this Part V . . . . □

				Yes	No
1a	Enter the number reported in box 3 of Form 1096. Enter -0- if not applicable	**1a**			
b	Enter the number of Forms W-2G included on line 1a. Enter -0- if not applicable . . .	**1b**			
c	Did the organization comply with backup withholding rules for reportable payments to vendors and reportable gaming (gambling) winnings to prize winners?		**1c**		

Form 990 (2023)

Part V Statements Regarding Other IRS Filings and Tax Compliance *(continued)*

			Yes	No
2a	Enter the number of employees reported on Form W-3, Transmittal of Wage and Tax Statements, filed for the calendar year ending with or within the year covered by this return **2a**			
b	If at least one is reported on line 2a, did the organization file all required federal employment tax returns? .	**2b**		
3a	Did the organization have unrelated business gross income of $1,000 or more during the year?	**3a**		
b	If "Yes," has it filed a Form 990-T for this year? *If "No" to line 3b, provide an explanation on Schedule O* .	**3b**		
4a	At any time during the calendar year, did the organization have an interest in, or a signature or other authority over, a financial account in a foreign country (such as a bank account, securities account, or other financial account)?	**4a**		
b	If "Yes," enter the name of the foreign country _____ See instructions for filing requirements for FinCEN Form 114, Report of Foreign Bank and Financial Accounts (FBAR).			
5a	Was the organization a party to a prohibited tax shelter transaction at any time during the tax year? . .	**5a**		
b	Did any taxable party notify the organization that it was or is a party to a prohibited tax shelter transaction?	**5b**		
c	If "Yes" to line 5a or 5b, did the organization file Form 8886-T?	**5c**		
6a	Does the organization have annual gross receipts that are normally greater than $100,000, and did the organization solicit any contributions that were not tax deductible as charitable contributions?	**6a**		
b	If "Yes," did the organization include with every solicitation an express statement that such contributions or gifts were not tax deductible?	**6b**		
7	**Organizations that may receive deductible contributions under section 170(c).**			
a	Did the organization receive a payment in excess of $75 made partly as a contribution and partly for goods and services provided to the payor?	**7a**		
b	If "Yes," did the organization notify the donor of the value of the goods or services provided?	**7b**		
c	Did the organization sell, exchange, or otherwise dispose of tangible personal property for which it was required to file Form 8282?	**7c**		
d	If "Yes," indicate the number of Forms 8282 filed during the year **7d**			
e	Did the organization receive any funds, directly or indirectly, to pay premiums on a personal benefit contract?	**7e**		
f	Did the organization, during the year, pay premiums, directly or indirectly, on a personal benefit contract? .	**7f**		
g	If the organization received a contribution of qualified intellectual property, did the organization file Form 8899 as required?	**7g**		
h	If the organization received a contribution of cars, boats, airplanes, or other vehicles, did the organization file a Form 1098-C?	**7h**		
8	**Sponsoring organizations maintaining donor advised funds.** Did a donor advised fund maintained by the sponsoring organization have excess business holdings at any time during the year?	**8**		
9	**Sponsoring organizations maintaining donor advised funds.**			
a	Did the sponsoring organization make any taxable distributions under section 4966?	**9a**		
b	Did the sponsoring organization make a distribution to a donor, donor advisor, or related person? . . .	**9b**		
10	**Section 501(c)(7) organizations.** Enter:			
a	Initiation fees and capital contributions included on Part VIII, line 12 . . . . **10a**			
b	Gross receipts, included on Form 990, Part VIII, line 12, for public use of club facilities . **10b**			
11	**Section 501(c)(12) organizations.** Enter:			
a	Gross income from members or shareholders **11a**			
b	Gross income from other sources. (Do not net amounts due or paid to other sources against amounts due or received from them.) **11b**			
12a	**Section 4947(a)(1) non-exempt charitable trusts.** Is the organization filing Form 990 in lieu of Form 1041?	**12a**		
b	If "Yes," enter the amount of tax-exempt interest received or accrued during the year . . **12b**			
13	**Section 501(c)(29) qualified nonprofit health insurance issuers.**			
a	Is the organization licensed to issue qualified health plans in more than one state?	**13a**		
	Note: See the instructions for additional information the organization must report on Schedule O.			
b	Enter the amount of reserves the organization is required to maintain by the states in which the organization is licensed to issue qualified health plans **13b**			
c	Enter the amount of reserves on hand **13c**			
14a	Did the organization receive any payments for indoor tanning services during the tax year?	**14a**		
b	If "Yes," has it filed a Form 720 to report these payments? *If "No," provide an explanation on Schedule O* .	**14b**		
15	Is the organization subject to the section 4960 tax on payment(s) of more than $1,000,000 in remuneration or excess parachute payment(s) during the year?	**15**		
	If "Yes," see the instructions and file Form 4720, Schedule N.			
16	Is the organization an educational institution subject to the section 4968 excise tax on net investment income?	**16**		
	If "Yes," complete Form 4720, Schedule O.			
17	**Section 501(c)(21) organizations.** Did the trust, or any disqualified or other person, engage in any activities that would result in the imposition of an excise tax under section 4951, 4952, or 4953?	**17**		
	If "Yes," complete Form 6069.			

Form **990** (2023)

Page **6**

Part VI	Governance, Management, and Disclosure. *For each "Yes" response to lines 2 through 7b below, and for a "No" response to line 8a, 8b, or 10b below, describe the circumstances, processes, or changes on Schedule O. See instructions.*

Check if Schedule O contains a response or note to any line in this Part VI . . . . ☐

Section A. Governing Body and Management

			Yes	No
1a	Enter the number of voting members of the governing body at the end of the tax year . .	1a		
	If there are material differences in voting rights among members of the governing body, or if the governing body delegated broad authority to an executive committee or similar committee, explain on Schedule O.			
b	Enter the number of voting members included on line 1a, above, who are independent .	1b		
2	Did any officer, director, trustee, or key employee have a family relationship or a business relationship with any other officer, director, trustee, or key employee?	2		
3	Did the organization delegate control over management duties customarily performed by or under the direct supervision of officers, directors, trustees, or key employees to a management company or other person? .	3		
4	Did the organization make any significant changes to its governing documents since the prior Form 990 was filed?	4		
5	Did the organization become aware during the year of a significant diversion of the organization's assets? .	5		
6	Did the organization have members or stockholders?	6		
7a	Did the organization have members, stockholders, or other persons who had the power to elect or appoint one or more members of the governing body?	7a		
b	Are any governance decisions of the organization reserved to (or subject to approval by) members, stockholders, or persons other than the governing body?	7b		
8	Did the organization contemporaneously document the meetings held or written actions undertaken during the year by the following:			
a	The governing body?	8a		
b	Each committee with authority to act on behalf of the governing body?	8b		
9	Is there any officer, director, trustee, or key employee listed in Part VII, Section A, who cannot be reached at the organization's mailing address? *If "Yes," provide the names and addresses on Schedule O*	9		

Section B. Policies *(This Section B requests information about policies not required by the Internal Revenue Code.)*

			Yes	No
10a	Did the organization have local chapters, branches, or affiliates?	10a		
b	If "Yes," did the organization have written policies and procedures governing the activities of such chapters, affiliates, and branches to ensure their operations are consistent with the organization's exempt purposes?	10b		
11a	Has the organization provided a complete copy of this Form 990 to all members of its governing body before filing the form?	11a		
b	Describe on Schedule O the process, if any, used by the organization to review this Form 990.			
12a	Did the organization have a written conflict of interest policy? *If "No," go to line 13*	12a		
b	Were officers, directors, or trustees, and key employees required to disclose annually interests that could give rise to conflicts?	12b		
c	Did the organization regularly and consistently monitor and enforce compliance with the policy? *If "Yes," describe on Schedule O how this was done*	12c		
13	Did the organization have a written whistleblower policy?	13		
14	Did the organization have a written document retention and destruction policy?	14		
15	Did the process for determining compensation of the following persons include a review and approval by independent persons, comparability data, and contemporaneous substantiation of the deliberation and decision?			
a	The organization's CEO, Executive Director, or top management official	15a		
b	Other officers or key employees of the organization	15b		
	If "Yes" to line 15a or 15b, describe the process on Schedule O. See instructions.			
16a	Did the organization invest in, contribute assets to, or participate in a joint venture or similar arrangement with a taxable entity during the year?	16a		
b	If "Yes," did the organization follow a written policy or procedure requiring the organization to evaluate its participation in joint venture arrangements under applicable federal tax law, and take steps to safeguard the organization's exempt status with respect to such arrangements?	16b		

Section C. Disclosure

17	List the states with which a copy of this Form 990 is required to be filed
18	Section 6104 requires an organization to make its Forms 1023 (1024 or 1024-A, if applicable), 990, and 990-T (section 501(c)(3)s only) available for public inspection. Indicate how you made these available. Check all that apply.
	☐ Own website ☐ Another's website ☐ Upon request ☐ Other *(explain on Schedule O)*
19	Describe on Schedule O whether (and if so, how) the organization made its governing documents, conflict of interest policy, and financial statements available to the public during the tax year.
20	State the name, address, and telephone number of the person who possesses the organization's books and records.

Form **990** (2023)

Form 990 (2023)   Page **7**

Part VII Compensation of Officers, Directors, Trustees, Key Employees, Highest Compensated Employees, and Independent Contractors

Check if Schedule O contains a response or note to any line in this Part VII . . . . □

Section A. Officers, Directors, Trustees, Key Employees, and Highest Compensated Employees

1a Complete this table for all persons required to be listed. Report compensation for the calendar year ending with or within the organization's tax year.

• List all of the organization's **current** officers, directors, trustees (whether individuals or organizations), regardless of amount of compensation. Enter -0- in columns (D), (E), and (F) if no compensation was paid.

• List all of the organization's **current** key employees, if any. See the instructions for definition of "key employee."

• List the organization's five **current** highest compensated employees (other than an officer, director, trustee, or key employee) who received reportable compensation (box 5 of Form W-2, box 6 of Form 1099-MISC, and/or box 1 of Form 1099-NEC) of more than $100,000 from the organization and any related organizations.

• List all of the organization's **former** officers, key employees, and highest compensated employees who received more than $100,000 of reportable compensation from the organization and any related organizations.

• List all of the organization's **former directors or trustees** that received, in the capacity as a former director or trustee of the organization, more than $10,000 of reportable compensation from the organization and any related organizations.

See the instructions for the order in which to list the persons above.

□ Check this box if neither the organization nor any related organization compensated any current officer, director, or trustee.

(A) Name and title	(B) Average hours per week (list any hours for related organizations below dotted line)	(C) Position (do not check more than one box, unless person is both an officer and a director/trustee)						(D) Reportable compensation from the organization (W-2/ 1099-MISC/ 1099-NEC)	(E) Reportable compensation from related organizations (W-2/ 1099-MISC/ 1099-NEC)	(F) Estimated amount of other compensation from the organization and related organizations
		Individual trustee or director	Institutional trustee	Officer	Key employee	Highest compensated employee	Former			
(1)										
(2)										
(3)										
(4)										
(5)										
(6)										
(7)										
(8)										
(9)										
(10)										
(11)										
(12)										
(13)										
(14)										

Form **990** (2023)

Form 990 (2023)
Page **8**

Part VII Section A. Officers, Directors, Trustees, Key Employees, and Highest Compensated Employees *(continued)*

(A) Name and title	(B) Average hours per week (list any hours for related organizations below dotted line)	(C) Position (do not check more than one box, unless person is both an officer and a director/trustee)						(D) Reportable compensation from the organization (W-2/ 1099-MISC/ 1099-NEC)	(E) Reportable compensation from related organizations (W-2/ 1099-MISC/ 1099-NEC)	(F) Estimated amount of other compensation from the organization and related organizations
		Individual trustee or director	Institutional trustee	Officer	Key employee	Highest compensated employee	Former			
(15)										
(16)										
(17)										
(18)										
(19)										
(20)										
(21)										
(22)										
(23)										
(24)										
(25)										

1b Subtotal . . . . ▶
  c Total from continuation sheets to Part VII, Section A . . . . . ▶
  d Total (add lines 1b and 1c) . . . . ▶

2 Total number of individuals (including but not limited to those listed above) who received more than $100,000 of reportable compensation from the organization ▶

		Yes	No
3	Did the organization list any **former** officer, director, trustee, key employee, or highest compensated employee on line 1a? If "Yes," complete Schedule J for such individual **3**		
4	For any individual listed on line 1a, is the sum of reportable compensation and other compensation from the organization and related organizations greater than $150,000? If "Yes," complete Schedule J for such individual **4**		
5	Did any person listed on line 1a receive or accrue compensation from any unrelated organization or individual for services rendered to the organization? If "Yes," complete Schedule J for such person **5**		

Section B. Independent Contractors

1 Complete this table for your five highest compensated independent contractors that received more than $100,000 of compensation from the organization. Report compensation for the calendar year ending with or within the organization's tax year.

(A) Name and business address	(B) Description of services	(C) Compensation

2 Total number of independent contractors (including but not limited to those listed above) who received more than $100,000 of compensation from the organization ▶

Form **990** (2023)

Part VIII   Statement of Revenue

Check if Schedule O contains a response or note to any line in this Part VIII . . . . ☐

				(A) Total revenue	(B) Related or exempt function revenue	(C) Unrelated business revenue	(D) Revenue excluded from tax under sections 512–514
Contributions, Gifts, Grants, and Other Similar Amounts	1a	Federated campaigns	1a				
	b	Membership dues	1b				
	c	Fundraising events	1c				
	d	Related organizations	1d				
	e	Government grants (contributions)	1e				
	f	All other contributions, gifts, grants, and similar amounts not included above	1f				
	g	Noncash contributions included in lines 1a–1f	1g	$			
	h	**Total.** Add lines 1a–1f					
Program Service Revenue	2a	_____	Business Code				
	b	_____					
	c	_____					
	d	_____					
	e	_____					
	f	All other program service revenue . .					
	g	**Total.** Add lines 2a–2f					
Other Revenue	3	Investment income (including dividends, interest, and other similar amounts)					
	4	Income from investment of tax-exempt bond proceeds					
	5	Royalties					
	6a	Gross rents . .	(i) Real		(ii) Personal			
			6a					
	b	Less: rental expenses	6b					
	c	Rental income or (loss)	6c					
	d	Net rental income or (loss)					
	7a	Gross amount from sales of assets other than inventory	(i) Securities		(ii) Other			
			7a					
	b	Less: cost or other basis and sales expenses .	7b					
	c	Gain or (loss) . .	7c					
	d	Net gain or (loss)					
	8a	Gross income from fundraising events (not including $_____ of contributions reported on line 1c). See Part IV, line 18 . . .	8a				
	b	Less: direct expenses	8b				
	c	Net income or (loss) from fundraising events . . .					
	9a	Gross income from gaming activities. See Part IV, line 19 .	9a				
	b	Less: direct expenses	9b				
	c	Net income or (loss) from gaming activities					
	10a	Gross sales of inventory, less returns and allowances . . .	10a				
	b	Less: cost of goods sold . . .	10b				
	c	Net income or (loss) from sales of inventory					
Miscellaneous Revenue	11a	_____	Business Code				
	b	_____					
	c	_____					
	d	All other revenue					
	e	**Total.** Add lines 11a–11d					
	12	**Total revenue.** See instructions					

Form **990** (2023)

Form 990 (2023)   Page **10**

| **Part IX** | **Statement of Functional Expenses** |

Section 501(c)(3) and 501(c)(4) organizations must complete all columns. All other organizations must complete column (A).

Check if Schedule O contains a response or note to any line in this Part IX . . . . ☐

Do not include amounts reported on lines 6b, 7b, 8b, 9b, and 10b of Part VIII.	(A) Total expenses	(B) Program service expenses	(C) Management and general expenses	(D) Fundraising expenses
1 Grants and other assistance to domestic organizations and domestic governments. See Part IV, line 21 .				
2 Grants and other assistance to domestic individuals. See Part IV, line 22				
3 Grants and other assistance to foreign organizations, foreign governments, and foreign individuals. See Part IV, lines 15 and 16				
4 Benefits paid to or for members				
5 Compensation of current officers, directors, trustees, and key employees				
6 Compensation not included above to disqualified persons (as defined under section 4958(f)(1)) and persons described in section 4958(c)(3)(B) . .				
7 Other salaries and wages				
8 Pension plan accruals and contributions (include section 401(k) and 403(b) employer contributions)				
9 Other employee benefits				
10 Payroll taxes				
11 Fees for services (nonemployees):				
a Management				
b Legal				
c Accounting				
d Lobbying				
e Professional fundraising services. See Part IV, line 17				
f Investment management fees				
g Other. (If line 11g amount exceeds 10% of line 25, column (A), amount, list line 11g expenses on Schedule O.) .				
12 Advertising and promotion				
13 Office expenses				
14 Information technology				
15 Royalties				
16 Occupancy				
17 Travel				
18 Payments of travel or entertainment expenses for any federal, state, or local public officials				
19 Conferences, conventions, and meetings .				
20 Interest				
21 Payments to affiliates				
22 Depreciation, depletion, and amortization .				
23 Insurance				
24 Other expenses. Itemize expenses not covered above. (List miscellaneous expenses on line 24e. If line 24e amount exceeds 10% of line 25, column (A), amount, list line 24e expenses on Schedule O.)				
a _____				
b _____				
c _____				
d _____				
e All other expenses				
25 **Total functional expenses.** Add lines 1 through 24e				
26 **Joint costs.** Complete this line only if the organization reported in column (B) joint costs from a combined educational campaign and fundraising solicitation. Check here ☐ if following SOP 98-2 (ASC 958-720) . . .				

Form **990** (2023)

	Part X	**Balance Sheet**			
		Check if Schedule O contains a response or note to any line in this Part X . . . . ☐			
				(A) Beginning of year	**(B)** End of year
Assets	1	Cash—non-interest-bearing	**1**		
	2	Savings and temporary cash investments	**2**		
	3	Pledges and grants receivable, net	**3**		
	4	Accounts receivable, net	**4**		
	5	Loans and other receivables from any current or former officer, director, trustee, key employee, creator or founder, substantial contributor, or 35% controlled entity or family member of any of these persons	**5**		
	6	Loans and other receivables from other disqualified persons (as defined under section 4958(f)(1)), and persons described in section 4958(c)(3)(B)	**6**		
	7	Notes and loans receivable, net	**7**		
	8	Inventories for sale or use	**8**		
	9	Prepaid expenses and deferred charges	**9**		
	10a	Land, buildings, and equipment: cost or other basis. Complete Part VI of Schedule D . . . **10a**			
	b	Less: accumulated depreciation **10b**	**10c**		
	11	Investments—publicly traded securities	**11**		
	12	Investments—other securities. See Part IV, line 11	**12**		
	13	Investments—program-related. See Part IV, line 11	**13**		
	14	Intangible assets	**14**		
	15	Other assets. See Part IV, line 11	**15**		
	16	**Total assets.** Add lines 1 through 15 (must equal line 33)	**16**		
Liabilities	17	Accounts payable and accrued expenses	**17**		
	18	Grants payable	**18**		
	19	Deferred revenue	**19**		
	20	Tax-exempt bond liabilities	**20**		
	21	Escrow or custodial account liability. Complete Part IV of Schedule D .	**21**		
	22	Loans and other payables to any current or former officer, director, trustee, key employee, creator or founder, substantial contributor, or 35% controlled entity or family member of any of these persons	**22**		
	23	Secured mortgages and notes payable to unrelated third parties . .	**23**		
	24	Unsecured notes and loans payable to unrelated third parties . . .	**24**		
	25	Other liabilities (including federal income tax, payables to related third parties, and other liabilities not included on lines 17–24). Complete Part X of Schedule D	**25**		
	26	**Total liabilities.** Add lines 17 through 25	**26**		
Net Assets or Fund Balances		**Organizations that follow FASB ASC 958, check here** ☐ **and complete lines 27, 28, 32, and 33.**			
	27	Net assets without donor restrictions	**27**		
	28	Net assets with donor restrictions	**28**		
		Organizations that do not follow FASB ASC 958, check here ☐ **and complete lines 29 through 33.**			
	29	Capital stock or trust principal, or current funds	**29**		
	30	Paid-in or capital surplus, or land, building, or equipment fund . . .	**30**		
	31	Retained earnings, endowment, accumulated income, or other funds .	**31**		
	32	Total net assets or fund balances	**32**		
	33	Total liabilities and net assets/fund balances	**33**		

Form 990 (2023) Page **12**

Part XI	**Reconciliation of Net Assets**		
	Check if Schedule O contains a response or note to any line in this Part XI . . . . ☐		
1	Total revenue (must equal Part VIII, column (A), line 12)	1	
2	Total expenses (must equal Part IX, column (A), line 25)	2	
3	Revenue less expenses. Subtract line 2 from line 1	3	
4	Net assets or fund balances at beginning of year (must equal Part X, line 32, column (A)) . . .	4	
5	Net unrealized gains (losses) on investments	5	
6	Donated services and use of facilities	6	
7	Investment expenses	7	
8	Prior period adjustments	8	
9	Other changes in net assets or fund balances (explain on Schedule O)	9	
10	Net assets or fund balances at end of year. Combine lines 3 through 9 (must equal Part X, line 32, column (B))	10	

Part XII	**Financial Statements and Reporting**			
	Check if Schedule O contains a response or note to any line in this Part XII . . . . ☐			
			Yes	No
1	Accounting method used to prepare the Form 990: ☐ Cash ☐ Accrual ☐ Other _____ If the organization changed its method of accounting from a prior year or checked "Other," explain on Schedule O.			
2a	Were the organization's financial statements compiled or reviewed by an independent accountant? . . .	2a		
	If "Yes," check a box below to indicate whether the financial statements for the year were compiled or reviewed on a separate basis, consolidated basis, or both.			
	☐ Separate basis ☐ Consolidated basis ☐ Both consolidated and separate basis			
b	Were the organization's financial statements audited by an independent accountant?	2b		
	If "Yes," check a box below to indicate whether the financial statements for the year were audited on a separate basis, consolidated basis, or both.			
	☐ Separate basis ☐ Consolidated basis ☐ Both consolidated and separate basis			
c	If "Yes" to line 2a or 2b, does the organization have a committee that assumes responsibility for oversight of the audit, review, or compilation of its financial statements and selection of an independent accountant? .	2c		
	If the organization changed either its oversight process or selection process during the tax year, explain on Schedule O.			
3a	As a result of a federal award, was the organization required to undergo an audit or audits as set forth in the Uniform Guidance, 2 C.F.R. Part 200, Subpart F?	3a		
b	If "Yes," did the organization undergo the required audit or audits? If the organization did not undergo the required audit or audits, explain why on Schedule O and describe any steps taken to undergo such audits .	3b		

Form **990** (2023)

Contact

To connect with author Rob Acton for media inquiries, speaking engagements, governance training, or to discuss a governance-related matter, visit www.robacton.com or reach out to rob@causestrategypartners.com.

Cause Strategy Partners works at the intersection of business and social impact to connect a diverse and talented network of professionals to nonprofit board service opportunities. We partner with the world's leading companies, professional services firms, and private foundations to help them advance their corporate social responsibility and leadership development goals, increase employee satisfaction, and create meaningful connections within the communities they serve.

Through our proprietary technology, innovative process, and team of experts, BoardLead matches potential governing board and young professional board candidates to carefully vetted nonprofits working in their cause area of interest. Through our BoardLearn platform and learning experiences, we train board members and board candidates to be highly effective in governance. Our Executive Concierge Board Placement service connects senior executives at top companies with board opportunities at high-profile nonprofits.

We are proud to be an award-winning Certified B-Corporation, part of a global community of companies that meet rigorous standards of performance, accountability, and transparency, committed to using the power of business to build strong local communities.

To learn more about how Rob Acton and Cause Strategy Partners are inspiring the world's professionals to serve their cause, visit www.causestrategypartners.com.

Printed in the USA
CPSIA information can be obtained
at www.ICGtesting.com
JSHW021233030824
67488JS00003B/6